"*Golf Inside the Zone* will help golfers, coaches, caddies and
mental side of the game. The book has an approachable, easy to understand and
practical interactive workbook style which will help the golfer be his/her best both on
and off the course."

  —**Dr. Alan Goldberg**, *Mental Training Coach, competitivedge.com*

"There is one truth that stands out more than any other and that is, the answers to
fluid, flowing and extraordinary performance lie within each of us to be discovered
when we are ready. To facilitate that journey within, Rob Polishook has written
the right book at the right time to help you go inside and learn the important lessons
that will transform your relationship not just with golf but with all of life. *Golf Inside the
Zone* will enable you to be the best version of yourself on and off the links."

  —**Jerry Lynch, Ph.D**, *Founder of wayofchampions.com,*
  author of 14 books including The Competitive Buddha.

"We practice our long game and our short game, but what about our mental game?
Standing over a 3-foot putt on the last hole to win a match, it's not technique that
is likely to let us down. It's the distance between our ears where that putt is made.
Golf Inside the Zone provides 32 mental exercises that you can incorporate into your
practice routine so the next time the pressure is on, you have the tools to succeed."

  —**John O'Sullivan**, *Founder, changingthegameproject.com*

"Golf Inside the Zone encourages golfers to "dig inside their skin" to reveal their game and optimal mental approach The book´s unique format includes quotes, principles, articles, and workouts which will empower all golfers to be their best."

—**Juan Marquine**, *Director of Golf School, Cantegril Country Club, Punta del Este, Uruguay*

"In golf, there is no defense to make up for a bad offense. There are no other teammates to make up for your off day. The best golfers in the world go several years without winning a golf tournament. Failure is inevitable. This all makes the focus on the mental side of golf that much more important. Learning to stay present and build from each day is an invaluable lesson you will learn from *Golf Inside the Zone.*"

—**Michael Buttacavoli**, *Professional Golfer*

"Working with Rob was a pivotal point in my junior golf career. One of the most important mental lessons I learned from Rob is the concept of "controllables and uncontrollables". This is not just something I put to use on the course but is something I use in my daily life. Rob's knowledge of the game but more importantly the brain, can help positively impact any person's golf game."

—**Skyler S.**, *Junior Golf Player*

Working with Rob helped me embrace the mental side of the game, many things have become clearer to me especially when I play in local tournaments. My pre-shot routine has made me more relaxed. Learning to breathe and not get ahead of myself has calmed those first tee jitters. Now when a poor shot creeps in, I know how to let it go and stay in the moment. I no longer berate myself and am more patient.

Camila T., *Junior Golf Player*

"Until I met Rob, I would allow my emotions during play to almost always turn negative thoughts. He taught me how to treat my emotional energy (which is part of who I am) as a friend, mitigate the negative thoughts and turn the energy to positive. I play golf and tennis in age group competitions. Since working with Rob I have achieved a national ranking in tennis and won a local golf tournament by making several critical putts. Thank you, Rob."-

Joe M., *Golfer*

"I played in a PGA Tour open qualifier recently. Took top 25 after shooting 73. Was in the mix thru 11 (top 3 get in), then a triple on the par 5 12th diminished me (or so I thought). This hole was particularly frustrating as I was chipping for eagle on the side of the green, easy up and down for birdie, and bladed the chip into the water. Was instantly torn.

The good news: When walking up to the 13 tee, I looked down at my golf ball to read the marks TSTE (Tides, Seasons, Turning of the Earth, from *The Legend of Bagger Vance*). I instantly had a mental timeout, regained myself, and came back into the present. Finishing -2 in my last few holes.

This finish, which "old me mindset" would not have been able to do, opened up an opportunity unforeseen. This was my first PGA qualifier, host to numerous tour players including PGA, and the Korn Ferry Tour. Not only did I compete against these guys, but I had an opportunity to beat each and every one of them.

After this qualifier I went back down to school to compete in my final qualifier before our first event. I came back, felt my feet breathing with the earth, fired a –3 round after 7 hours in the car, and stole that last spot for the tournament.

I am currently at the event, which is host to the best colleges in the country. We had our practice round today and instead of the usual practice rounds that most golfers do, I DID ME (which was interesting to see my coach's reaction whom didn't quite understand what I was doing, but I sure as hell did) I worked on my ability to stay in the moment, to be calm in almost a dream state. And I can't wait for the opportunity tomorrow!!! I'm ready, I feel ready.

One thing that has really helped in my work with Rob, has been looking back on my notes, reading out quotes, and almost feeling what I felt when I wrote them down. Excited for what's to come."

—**Kevin**, *Collegiate Golfer*

Golf
Inside the Zone

32 Mental Training Workouts for Champions

What if <u>one thing</u>
could change EVERYTHING…?

Game Changer!

By Rob Polishook, M.A., C.P.C.

Golf on the Brain

Cover Design by Kellie Patterson
Text Composition by John Reinhardt Book Design

GOLF INSIDE THE ZONE
32 Mental Training Workouts for Champions
All rights reserved

Published and Distributed by Inside the Zone Sports Performance Group
www.insidethezone.com
rob@insidethezone.com

ISBN: 978-0-9891862-6-1

Printed in the United States of America

Contents

How to Use This Book

*G*olf *Inside the Zone: 32 Mental Training Workouts for Champions* can be read and experienced in different ways. Initially, I suggest browsing through the table of contents to gain a broad overview. You will notice there are four sections: Off-course, Pre-round, Mid-round, and Post-round. Then browse the individual workouts; each one also has four components:

- Quotes from the pros.
- Principles which serve as a foundation.
- A mental training article.
- Interactive worksheet which ties the quotes, principles and article together.

These four components (quotes, principles, article and worksheet) create what I have coined a "Mental Training Workout." The goal of the workout is to experientially guide you through the mental training concept. I hope they help you to confidently and purposefully incorporate the mental side of golf into your approach on the course.

Now that you're familiar with the book's layout, I suggest you read the book in one of the following ways.

Start with a random section or specific workout that resonates with you. For example, maybe you're having trouble keeping yourself calm and relaxed before a round? Go to workout #10 OMG!…I'm Nervous! What Do I Do?—Five Ways to Work Through Pre-Round Jitters. After reading the quotes, principles and article, take some time to think about them, and ask yourself a few questions: What does this workout mean to me? How might it apply to my situation? How could I incorporate the principles into my game? If I did, what might happen? How and when will I do it? Lastly, pick up your pen and complete the mental training workout. Take your time and approach each workout with P.I.P. (purpose, intention, and passion). Each workout might take between 15 and 45 minutes to complete.

Golf Inside the Zone can also be experienced by simply reading and completing the workouts starting at Chapter 1 and going through the workouts in order, reflecting and highlighting the parts which resonate with you.

I suggest, choosing a partner and working through the workouts together. This is a great opportunity to share ideas.

Coaches, teachers, parents and sport psychology professionals can also facilitate the workouts in a group or team setting, encouraging golfers to self reflect and share their experiences. Maybe picking out the key points and how a golfer could implement the teaching.

What Are Mental Training Workouts?

Golf Inside the Zone: 32 Mental Training Workouts for Champions allows you, the golfer, coach or parent to seamlessly integrate the mental game into the physical game of golf. Dedicating time and discipline on the mental game will positively improve your overall performance on the course. Over the years, I have observed golfers who made time for drills on both the putting and driving range, practice rounds and off the course fitness focusing on flexibility, strength and conditioning. This same commitment and intention must be made for the mental game. It's the "glue" that holds everything together.

Golf Inside the Zone consists of 32 cutting-edge mental training "workouts." Each workout highlights a specific mental training principle such as focusing on what you can control, how to use imagery in preparing for each round, creating routines for yourself, or managing negative self-talk. Specifically, each workout includes quotes from the pros, key principles, an in-depth article, and an experiential interactive workout for the golfer to complete.

Improving a player's mental game takes time. It's a process during which the golfer will undoubtedly experience moments of feeling in control, moments of frustration, and moments where progress simply is not evident. In fact, it is much like making a swing change. It takes time to develop the proper form and get a feel for the motion. Then comes the development of controlling the club face at impact followed by building up enough confidence to implement it in competition. Each step builds on the previous one, like a growing tree: first come the seeds, then the roots, then the trunk, then the branches, then the leaves, and finally the fruits!

The discipline to allocate real time to complete a *workout* for the mental game demonstrates purpose, intention, and passion. Oftentimes, when a golfer works on the mental game it happens only after they played a round, drills, fitness, and school work are completed! In many cases, golfers, parents or coaches don't even think about the impact of the mental game until a bad round or three-putts mount. I know, because this is when most of my clients come to seek my mental training services. My phone rings like a fire alarm has gone off! In actuality, the loss, or struggle over the ball is not the problem, but a symptom of something else which is behind it.

By reading and completing the *workouts* in *Golf Inside the Zone* golfers, parents and coaches can follow a fun, systematic, and personally experiential approach to gain confidence in their mental game.

Golf Inside the Zone will help you discover your unique strengths and make them even more potent while identifying and moving beyond challenges, obstacles and blocks which get in the way of your peak performance. It will help you reflect on yourself as a person and a golfer and hone in on best practices for you as an individual. The book can be seen as a mirror, helping you to reflect on your experiences. Golf Inside the Zone can help you improve as a golfer on the range, the course, and in tournaments without even swinging a club!

It can help you:

- adapt and adjust from shot to shot or hole to hole.
- execute like you do in practice during your rounds.
- manage pressure, tension and slow the game down.
- stay focused on the moment and let go of distracting or uncontrollable factors.
- embrace challenges, pressure, and competition.

Who should read this book?

Golf Inside the Zone was written for golfers, however the concepts apply to all athletes of all sports. It will also serve coaches, caddies, parents, and even fans to help them understand and relate to what their golfer is experiencing and feeling. Additionally, it will provide valuable ideas to help them coach and support the individual golfer. The book provides practical value-added stories, quotes, exercises and worksheets to help golfers move forward in their journey toward achieving their personal peak performance. It will help you be the best version of yourself both on and off the course.

Why is this book different?

Golf Inside the Zone is an interactive book that is designed to engage the athlete and help them create a personal experience, one which will guide them beyond self-imposed limits, expectations, and mental blocks. Golf Inside the Zone will help the athlete become aware of what makes them unique and how to translate these attributes into their performance on the course.

Golf Inside the Zone was not written from an ivory tower; in fact, I like to say it's written from being right alongside my clients. The chapter ideas all came from my clients!

Golf Inside the Zone includes real examples, quotes, and stories from my clients' experiences; as well as observations from watching my clients golf. For example, how many of you have said, "I'm better, how could I play so bad?" or, "I'm nervous, what do I do?"

Most golfers spend very little time on the mental game. Maybe they read an article here or there or pick up a quote. But rarely do they have the opportunity to reflect and apply the information to each shot throughout their round. This book features stories, workouts, quotes from noted golfers and articles which highlight specific competitive situations to golf.

Golf Inside the Zone knows that you are more than an athlete, you are a whole human athlete. And your secret to personal peak performance is bringing who you are to what you do. Person first. Every time.

Get ready for a fun ride around the course.

The journey starts now…

Honing
the Craft—
See it,
Feel it,
Roll it…

Section 1
OFF-COURSE WORKOUTS

Off-Course Workouts

To the Child Within

*There's a child inside of you who holds the key to your greatest dreams.
While she may be sometimes frightened by other people and events, she refuses to let go of those dreams.
She tugs at your leg for attention.
She whines for you to notice her.
She whispers in your ear of all that you can be.
Sometimes you'd just like her to go away with all that silliness.
No such luck. She's too persistent.
She's determined to get noticed.
She refuses to give up.
You've tried to talk some reason into her, but thankfully she won't listen.
Others have told her the "facts" and the limits on what's possible.
She's not interested in their "impossible."
She does not understand "can't."
She doesn't care if others laugh at her dreams, as long as you don't.
She wants you to consider the possibilities.
She wants to show you what she can do.
She will not quit until she's gotten your attention.
Her spirit can't be broken.
She refuses to stay down.
Her resiliency is awe inspiring.
Her enthusiasm is refreshing and boundless.
Harness that child within.
Learn to listen to her.
Let her guide you to your dreams.*

—**Dr. Alan Goldberg**,
author of *Sports Slump Busting* and co-author of *This is Your Brain on Sports*

Workout 1
Mental Point

Athletes with the mental edge rise above adversity and adapt to what's happening in the present moment.

How Do I Get the Mental Edge?
Unlock the Mystery of the Mental Game

What the Pros Are Saying

"The whole secret to mastering the game of golf…is to cultivate a mental approach to the game that will enable you to shrug off the bad days, keep patient and know in your heart that sooner or later you will be back on top."

—**Arnold Palmer**, *Seven-time Major champion*

"I'm about five inches from being an outstanding golfer, the distance my left ear is from my right."

—**Ben Crenshaw**, *Two-time Masters champion*

"The mind is your greatest weapon. It's the greatest club in your bag. It's also your Achilles' heel."

—**Steve Elkington**, *One-time Major champion*

Key Principles

1. Focus on the process, not the outcome.
2. It's not *when* you get there, it's *how* you get there.
3. Redefine success beyond winning and losing—play proud, play hard and compete.

How Do I Get the Mental Edge?

Ask any athlete how important the mental game is—most would say it's between 50% and 99%. In an individual sport such as golf that importance always challenges the higher limits. Remember this quote from Hall of Fame golf instructor Jim Flick, "Golf is 90 percent mental and the other 10 percent is mental too." Many athletes don't understand how to unlock the mystery of the mental game. However, the first step begins by asking the right questions.

What is the mental edge?

Athletes with the mental edge rise above adversity. They also adapt and adjust to what is happening in the present moment. Key characteristics of the mental game include patience, calmness under pressure, focusing on what you can control, letting go of what you cannot control, and getting comfortable being uncomfortable. These athletes also have the ability to elevate their level when it's needed most. Think about the 2020 PGA Championship where Collin Morikawa was tied for the lead with six other golfers on the final back nine. He had the presence of mind to balance the risk and reward of attempting to drive the 16th green and it paid off with an eagle—earning him a two-stroke lead and ultimately the margin for his first Major victory.

Who has the mental edge?

Two of the greatest golfers of all-time come to mind. These icons are Jack Nicklaus and Tiger Woods. These golfers are two of the best to ever 'tee it up.' Jack and Tiger currently combine for 33 Majors! They are known for elevating their game and hitting clutch shots under pressure. Most importantly, they have both demonstrated a deep appreciation of the mental game and the ability to adjust to adversity. Both golfers are well known for their mental resiliency and maintaining the mental edge during competition.

When do you need the mental edge?

Performing under adversity is the true mark of a champion. This is the time the mental edge is imperative. Most golfers can win when they are playing well—they have the momentum and their confidence. However, the true champions are the ones who find a way to win when they are not playing their best. Athletes with the mental edge take little for granted, give a full effort, and trust their process no matter the score or situation.

Imagine hitting your best drive. You follow that with a chunked pitching wedge and you come up short of the green. Playing with the mental edge would mean you accept that poor swing, rebound from it, and refocus on your next shot. You have the choice: Are you going to walk up to the ball kicking yourself and being frustrated with what happened? Or are you going to let go of imperfection, make the adjustments needed, settle down, and chip the ball on the green? This is having the mental edge. Accepting mistakes, learning from them, and then adapting and adjusting.

Where does the mental edge come from?

The mental edge lies within each of us. It starts on the inside and can be cultivated on the outside by people and experiences. The key is to trust the process, do your best, and learn from mistakes, setbacks, and obstacles. The mental edge isn't something that is only built on a fairway, it also incorporates what you do off the course. Are you getting the proper amount of sleep? Are you being purposeful in your practice? Are you incorporating a meditation routine? These are just a few things that will help a golfer off the course. On the course, it's about each round of golf, each tournament, and each stroke that can help you gain awareness, insight, and knowledge of your game.

Why is the mental edge important?

Eleven-time Major champion, Walter Hagen once said, "You don't have the game you played last year or last week. You only have today's game. It may be far from your best, but it's all you've got. Harden your heart and make the best of it." It is important to play each round one stroke at a time, one hole at a time. Doing this helps you to be aware and present. The mental game is the glue that holds everything together. When you have it you exhibit flexibility in situations, accept imperfections, and work with what you have on that given day. The ability to stay calm and centered under pressure is imperative. Remember, a winning performance is rarely perfect; more often it is the *perfectly imperfect* shots that change the course of a competition. A great mental approach is the most surefire way to walk into competition with an advantage.

How do I get the mental edge?

This is the million-dollar question. We know that having the mental edge is a crucial component of any elite golfer's game. What many of us don't understand is that similar to confidence and success, the mental edge is a consequence of actions, behaviors, commitment, experience, and discipline—all of which are in your control as a golfer! Great golfers are very aware and trusting of themselves, their sport, and their own process. Much like going to the range, the practice green, or playing as many rounds as you can, gaining the mental edge takes patience and commitment. Oftentimes it's not about doing more and forcing a result, but rather letting go of imperfections, moving on to the next shot, and committing with purpose, intention, and a focus on what you can control.

How Do I Get the Mental Edge?

In your experience, how important is the mental game during each round?

(scale: 1 = not important; 10 = very important) _____

_____

Explain why you gave it this rating: _____

_____

WHAT does it mean to have the mental edge? _____

_____

_____

WHO demonstrates the mental edge? (What player or team?) _____

_____

WHEN is it necessary to have the mental edge? _____

_____

WHERE does the mental edge come from? _____

_____

WHY is the mental edge important? _____

_____

_____

_____

HOW do golfers get the mental edge? _____

_____

Understanding the above ... List three actions you could do right away to improve your mental game by 5%: _____

1. _____

2, _____

3. _____

What would you have to sacrifice? _____

_____

Is it worth it? If yes, when will you start? _____

What specifically would change in your performance? _____

_____

_____

**Imagine what it would look and feel like to play with the mental edge ...
Describe it:** _____

_____

_____

_____

_____

_____

_____

Workout 2
Mental Point

"The foundation is the person. How you play is a manifestation of yourself. Your philosophy of self, determines your philosophy of your game, including strongest and weakest points."

—Dr. David Grand

Winning Within
Whole Human Athlete. Person First

What the Pros Are Saying

"As soon as you realize who you are is way cooler than who you are trying to be… That's going to be one hell of a day."

—**Adam Schriber**, *Swing coach for Anthony Kim*

"You may know mechanics or some mechanics, but every player is different, the way you treat every player is different and people disregard that fact."

—**George Gankas**, *Professional swing coach*

"There's a thousand different ways my life could have gone after my dad passed, but it was the people around me—and their love and selflessness—that allowed me to develop into the player I am today."

—**Lanto Griffin**, *One-time PGA tour winner*

Key Principles

1. An athlete is more than "just" an athlete. They are a whole human athlete.
2. There is a person behind every swing.
3. The fruits are a result of the roots.

Winning Within

A golfer is a person first and an athlete second; a whole human athlete. This idea may seem obvious, since we are all born without a club in our hands, but it is easy to identify as just an athlete. When we first walked onto the course to play we didn't miraculously change identities—we were the same person. We still are that same person.

Look at some of the professional golfers you are familiar with. Brooks Koepka, in his younger playing days, took note of needing to mature as a person in order to reach to his fullest potential. On Michael Collins' show, America's Caddie, he said, "I was competitive ever since I was little, and sometimes, it backfired a little bit…I ran many steps of punishment workouts [in college]. That was something that needed to happen at the time, I needed to develop more as a human being than as a golfer."

It can be helpful to think of your development in sports, and in life, as a tree. A tree starts from a seed where the roots create a foundation, an anchor of sorts. The roots can be thought of as a person's values, belief system, cultural orientation, work ethic, and soul. Influential people in our lives, like our parents, coaches, friends, and extended family, play a role in how our roots grow. For example, by encouraging such traits as moral values, personal confidence, self-belief, personal resiliency, integrity, and self-empowerment,

a person will be better suited to face obstacles, setbacks, and life's challenges. Experiences, both positive and negative, that we encounter also influence and cultivate our development.

The stronger the root system, the stronger the physical trunk and the branches become. The fruits are always a result of the roots. However, unfortunately, these fruits (results) often garner more attention than the roots (process). Yet make no mistake, the development of an athlete's performance all starts from the roots.

The mark of a great player is their emotional resiliency. The great champions have all shown an ability to face adversity, not get overwhelmed by it and move forward. In 1998, PGA Lifetime Achievement Award Winner and Hall of Fame Golfer Sam Snead, said, "In golf, like in life, we are dealt with much adversity. It is in the 'comeback' that can truly define who we are as both an athlete, and more importantly, as a person. We must be able to dig deep and learn from each failure, experience, and challenge."

Now, think back to a time when you were having a poor practice or tournament. Maybe your swings weren't coming off as clean as usual or your putts weren't rolling where you aimed. Is it possible that period of being *a touch off* stemmed from something in your personal life? Maybe a rough day at school, an argument with a friend, parental expectations, or even anxiety about the upcoming tournament? Off-course issues and unrelated stresses can affect performance on the golf course.

While we all think that we can compartmentalize and only think of golf on the course, we all know other thoughts surface between shots. Awareness of the complexity of the person-player relationship will help you understand that you are not a robot! We are human beings who are affected by what happens in our day-to-day lives. Off-course stresses, experiences, and emotional and physical traumas oftentimes get suppressed in the mind, but the psychological scars remain. Even big-time pros, like Tiger Woods, Sergio Garcia, Greg Norman, and others, can attest to this.

Again, think back, can you remember walking off the course after a heartbreaking loss, feeling dejected and rattled? It could be a tournament where you felt you should have won, but lost your focus and sliced your tee shot into the woods or maybe you had a putt lip-out on the 18th hole. You could hear the crowd gasp, as your stomach clutched with embarrassment. Certainly, the next time you tee up, it is likely that the image of your previous sliced-drive will flash before your eyes like a shooting star. Your mind and body remember. The key is not attaching to that thought, rather notice the feelings and do not fight with the thought. This will allow them to pass like a cloud in the sky.

Lastly, imagine this: you strain your back during a tournament and must be sidelined from golf for two to four weeks. When you return, people ask how the back is. You reply like a warrior, "It feels great. Never felt better." However, in practice you are afraid to go all out swinging the club like you used to because of some underlying and lingering pain. Then, you adjust your swing a bit to alleviate the pain. After that, you go through a period of poor ball-striking. What's important to understand is that the body remembers any kind of physical trauma, especially injuries and surgeries. The body will try to protect itself from further injury recurrence by adjusting. Most athletes recover from injuries on a physical level, however, recovering from the mental scars are much more difficult. A truly aware golfer will understand that something is getting in their way, not run away from the emotions, rather work though them. Sometimes seeing a sport psychologist that understands the somatic side of the body and sports can help.

In summary, when a golfer walks onto the course they are still the same person and carry personal issues, experiences, and traumas with them. Being able to accept, process, and learn from such issues is what will help you move forward. It's not about trying to block your personal experiences out; you should allow them in and accept what happened. When a golfer can trust themselves enough to bring who they are to what they do, that's when growth happens! The fruits are a result of the roots.

Winning Within

What's your story? Golf Journey Line

Chronologically list key moments or experiences in your past that have influenced or shaped the golfer you currently are. Take into account both golf and non-golf related key moments such as: meaningful wins or losses which you learned from, interactions which may have been impactful, challenges, adversity, or obstacles which you over-came, injuries, inspirations, influences, and confidence builders. List these key moments in the order that they happened.

1. _____

_____

2. _____

_____

3. _____

_____

4. _____

_____

5. _____

_____

6. _____

_____

7. _____

_____

8. _____

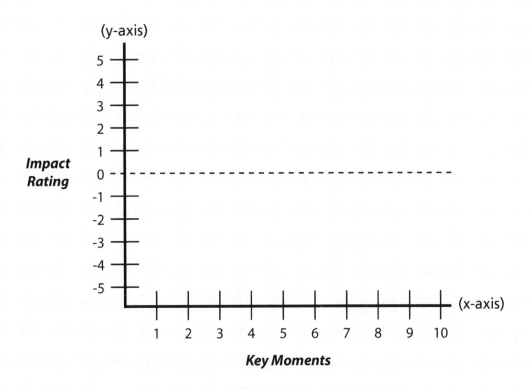

Plan your story ...

Plot the 8 key moments from above along the x-axis (start with the oldest events on the left). Then rate them in terms of impact, i.e. negative or positive, on the y-axis. Now, connect the dots to get a better picture of the ups and downs of your journey.

As you look at the graph depicting the highs and lows of your journey, what does the visual make you aware of?

_____

Remember the times you encountered adversity ... What did you learn from those experiences?

_____

Imagine the next five years: Describe what would you like to see.

_____

Workout 3
Mental Point

Overall, the "Big Why" is about motivation, empowerment, and purpose.

How to Get and Stay Motivated!
Understanding Your Big Why

What the Pros Are Saying

"Find something you love…When you love something, it tells you all its secrets."

—**Bob Parsons**, *Founder and CEO of PXG*

"I don't play the sport for fame. I don't try to win tournaments for fame…I don't do any of that. It's just me. I'm just Bubba. I goof around. I joke around."

—**Bubba Watson**, *Two-time Major Champion*

"One of the most fascinating things about golf is how it reflects the cycle of life. No matter what you shoot, the next day you have to go back to the first tee and begin all over again and make yourself into something."

—**Peter Jacobsen**, *Seven-time PGA Tour Winner, two-time Champions Tour Winner*

Key Principles

1. The "Big Why" has nothing to do with outcome.
2. The "Big Why" is the motivation to success.
3. The "Big Why" is what fuels an athlete.

How to Get and Stay Motivated!

Identifying and connecting to your "Big Why" may be the most important part of developing your mental game. Understanding the answer to these basic questions is imperative: Why do you play? What is it about the game of golf that you love? What are you willing to sacrifice to improve? When a player has a clearly defined "Big Why" they become better able to learn from mistakes, bounce back from failure, and play with purpose. Their "Big Why" is ultimately like a compass, always helping to keep them on track no matter the results.

Oftentimes, when conducting a workshop with a group of young golfers, I will bring a volunteer to the front and ask them to jump as high as they can from a standing position. Each time I'll ask them if they can jump higher then before. After a few jumps, the golfer usually says, "That's the highest I can go." I'll urge the golfer to try once more, only to hear the resignation in their voice, and hear the reply "I can't go any higher." It's at this point, that I will introduce some extra motivation—a reward that is meaningful to them. Proposing that if they can jump 2 inches higher, the reward is theirs! Sure enough, in the thousand or so times I have done this demonstration, the golfer always strategizes differently, pushes further, and resets with a higher level of intensity. The result, time and time again, is that the golfer surpasses the mark they earlier did not think they could reach.

After experiencing this exercise, the golfer immediately becomes self-aware of their increased motivation and sharper focus, which enabled them to strive higher and reach for more. Certainly, offering a prize as motivation is short-lived and at best provides short-term motivation. However, what is important is demonstrating how a golfer can achieve and accomplish more if they have an intrinsic "Big Why." When the "Big Why" is personal and individual, an athlete will feel lasting ownership, self-empowerment, and responsibility for their performance.

Arnold Palmer, seven-time Major winner, known for his competitive spirit once said, "I've always made a total effort, even when the odds seemed entirely against me. I never quit trying; I never felt that I didn't have a chance to win." Palmer's drive, determination, and willingness to bounce back carried him to become one of the greatest golfers to ever play the game. One could say Palmer's "Big Why" was his love of the game, the challenge, and the competition. Palmer knew the importance of the mental side of golf, saying, "Success in golf depends less on strength of body than upon strength of mind and character." His longtime rival, Jack Nicklaus, backs this up by saying, "Focus on remedies, not faults."

Understanding your "Big Why" is what will help you play purposeful and be the best version of yourself. This is one of the keys which separate one golfer from another.

Once a player identifies their "Big Why" it becomes important to plan measurable and realistic process-driven strategies in order to reach their goals. During this stage the athlete must recognize that they have choices and responsibilities in owning their success. Players should understand that they can take two roads. The first road is called the champions road. It is difficult and requires sacrifice, hard work, thousands of balls hit at the range, and it will include frustration and failure along the way. However, the reward will be personally satisfying. The second road is easy. It requires little work, no sacrifice, and it's a comfortable path that inspires minimal effort. This road leads an athlete to a place called "La-La-Land."

Often, I'll ask golfers to articulate and journal what they see each road looking like. I ask them to take many things into consideration when planning their roadmaps. The athletes should be looking at what choices, actions, and behaviors are necessary for each road. Athletes need to focus on how these different actions impact their family life, schoolwork, social life, and ultimately performance on the golf course. The biggest lesson is that the golfers realize their actions directly impact the results. It becomes obvious which road they are following: The Champions Road or straight to "La-La-Land!"

The "Big Why" is personal. It's about motivation, empowerment, and purpose. Recognizing how your actions and motivation affect the outcome is what differentiates an elite athlete from someone who just has natural talent. Cultivating an ath-

"Working hard for something we don't care about is called stress; working hard for something we love is called passion."

lete's "Big Why" will raise a golfer's mental game to the next level where concentration, awareness, and the emotional management become the focus. Embracing your "Big Why" means rethinking motivation by putting the expectations of others aside, and taking responsibility for your own game where you can optimize your unique personal strengths. Ultimately, the payoff for developing a "Big Why" is reaching unlimited potential, which in turn, impacts every area of a golfer's life.

How to Get and Stay Motivated!

The Big Why is an athlete's key secret to success.

When a golfer has an internally driven "Big Why" (reason for playing), which is not solely based on winning and losing, they will be more apt to persevere and focus on their process. This "Big Why" will enable them to strive and reach their personal peak potential.

List four reasons you enjoy playing golf (Big Why).

1. _____
2. _____
3. _____
4. _____

Now, considering the above Big Whys, rank them in order of importance:

1. _____
2. _____
3. _____
4. _____

Being aware of your Big Whys, how can they help to motivate you?

_____

_____

_____

_____

By playing golf, is there a person, player, coach, or team, which you hope to inspire or impact? Explain:

_____

_____

_____

What "character strengths" do you get back from playing golf?

_____

_____

_____

What's your overall goal as a golfer?

_____

_____

_____

What's your Big Why?

Workout 4
Mental Point

The tenets of competeology will help you stay present instead of worrying about results, the past, or looking ahead.

Competeology
The Key to Winning

What the Pros Are Saying

"He is very in control of all parts of his game, and on that Sunday that was really apparent. He has played for years and won many times on other tours, and he seemed very comfortable and confident in that situation. He just seemed like a guy who knew how to play within himself and hit the shots he needed to."

—**Maverick McNeal**, *PGA Tour rookie, speaking on José de Jesús Rodríguez*

"If I've got a swing, I've got a shot."

—**Bubba Watson**, *Two-time Masters Champion*

"I came away with a better understanding of what the game is about, and one thing is that you can't be afraid to lose. You have to put yourself in that position because it's the only way you'll ever win."

—**Greg Norman**, *Two-time Major Champion and #1ranked golfer for 331 weeks*

Key Principles

1. Adapting and adjusting are key components of competing.
2. It's not whether you make mistakes, but how quickly you can learn from them.
3. Define success based on objectives of improvement, not what the scoreboard says.

Competeology

Did you know that the suffix – "ology" means 'the study of?' For example, astrology is the study of stars and neurology is the study of the nervous system. So, what does all of this have to do with golf? Here, I will welcome you into the world of a new "ology," competeology: the study of competing. Competeology is what will help elevate the top golfers from the rest. Having that understanding of how to compete is the key to consistency and long-term success.

So, why is competeology so important? Think of it this way: We require a basic knowledge of all the different sciences to understand the world we live in, right? So, having an understanding of how to compete, and what it means to compete, would help give you a better understanding while actually playing. Competeology will give you the tools necessary to maximize your potential.

Being successful in golf can be defined by the golfer's ability to consistently make proper adjustments. Each course has its own slope and course rating. Obstacles, such as narrow fairways, thick rough, pin placements, etc., pose a challenge on each hole. Being able to navigate these obstacles and make the proper adjustments will help you to play better. Competeology turns a golfer into a student. It allows the athlete to learn as they make the necessary adjustments to put themselves in the best position to be successful. This turns each swing of a club into a lesson. Nine-time major champion Ben Hogan once said, "I never played a round when I didn't learn something new about the game."

By successfully utilizing the eight tenets of Competeology that are discussed below, you can earn your Ph.D. in Competeology. More importantly, this applied degree will position you to become the best version of yourself both on and off the course.

1. Cultivate a growth-based attitude vs. a fixed attitude

Carol Dweck, in her book Mindset, states that a competitor would always display a growth attitude. Competitors understand that their development is a process and while a poorly struck putt or shot into the water may be costly, there are lessons that can be learned. Competitive players view mistakes and failures as an opportunity to grow and develop. They understand the process and make adjustments to prepare themselves for their next opportunity. Suppose you tee up on a par 5 and you slice one into the woods—a golfer with a fixed mentality sees their skill level as unchangeable and gets exceedingly frustrated with their setbacks. Their mistake becomes the focal point and they begin to spiral out of control. However, a competitive golfer questions what they did wrong and makes the adjustments needed, setting the stage for future successes and even more positive development.

2. Focus on what you can control and let go of the rest

A competitive golfer stays focused on what they can control: things such as effort, energy, and bouncing back from adversity – to name a few. In golf, you cannot control the weather, you cannot control a bad bounce, or how well your opponent is playing. Being able to stay in the growth mindset becomes more and more critical because it allows you to stay focused on what you can control and bounce back from. Your reactions, adjustments, and ability to follow through with your process are all things that are in your hands! When a golfer can focus on their own game, execute their own game plan, and make the proper adjustments with each swing of the club, they can walk away knowing they did their best that day.

3. Adapt and adjust to situations

A competitor is constantly adjusting and adapting each time they address the ball. In golf, even the slightest adjustments can make a difference. What's most important is to acknowledge what is happening and bring your attention to aspects of your game that you can control. Too often, in pressure moments throughout a round, golfers will get caught up solely on their results. Focusing completely on a result will create anxiety and tension, because the golfer's main focus is on something that is outside of their control. The singular focus takes them away from a key question: What can I do now, in this moment, that I can control, that puts me in the best position to be successful?

4. Learn from mistakes

Eleven-time major winner Walter Hagen once said, "I expect to make at least seven mistakes a round. Therefore, when I make a bad shot, I don't worry about it. It is just one of those seven." Walter Hagen understood that mistakes are a part of the game; bad shots will happen. In golf, failure should be expected, encouraged, and most importantly, used as a stepping-stone towards your growth and development as a golfer. Ben Hogan said, "the most important shot in golf, is the next one." Mistakes and failure, in the game of golf, become problems only if the golfer does not learn from them.

5. Never, ever, ever, give up

Competing means never giving up. A competitive golfer accepts adversity and views those bad days as a challenge. A competitive golfer also doesn't mind winning a tournament on one last putt, or from having to come back from a few strokes down even if they did not play their best. They have perspective and they understand that every shot throughout each round is a new shot and what happens next is the most important thing.

6. Get comfortable being uncomfortable

Jason Day, former world number one, said, "Everyone has an uncomfortable club in their bag." A competitive golfer understands that there are moments throughout a round where they might have to take a calculated risk or step outside of the comfort of their game plan in order to be successful. As a result of these adjustments, the competitive golfer will push themselves, focusing on the present situation. They understand that by embracing the idea of getting comfortable being uncomfortable, they will become more resilient, and their game will become stronger, ultimately helping them reach another level.

7. Be aware and make high-percentage choices

In golf, we often draw a parallel of making high-percentage choices to discipline. For example, a disciplined golfer stays in-tune with their game, remaining focused on their shots and making the right decisions for each swing. The competitive golfer makes the smart plays, based on the situation in the tournament. You could be leading by a few strokes going into the final hole, which has a severe dogleg to the right. There might be a small window to attempt a drive through tree branches to cut off the dogleg, but doing this would create a much larger risk and could potentially lead to a double bogey. The competitive golfer would be aware of the score and know that laying up short and playing the dogleg conservatively would be the less riskier play. This helps ensure that they remain competitive and would give them the best shot at winning. Being aware of your options and choices are often what separates the winners from the others.

8. Sportsmanship

A competitor respects themselves, their opponent, the course, and the game itself. The focus is on playing hard and keeping the focus on what they can control. They play with integrity and honesty and recognizes that the field is not the enemy, and neither is the course. Rather they both can be thought of as partners. Partners to challenge the competitive golfer to be their best.

By following the above tenets of Competeology, you will put yourself in the best situation to succeed on the course. These concepts are all within a golfer's control, and practicing them will increase confidence throughout each round. They will help you to stay present in the moment instead of worrying about the results, focusing on the past, or looking ahead to the future. Lastly, they will help you manage adversity while playing. Ultimately, following the tenets of competeology will free you to learn and develop every time you step onto the course.

Competeology

com·pete (kə m·pēt'): 1. from late Latin competere: to strive together, meet, come together, agree; from com- [together] + petere [to seek]; 2. to enter into or be in rivalry; contend; vie (in a contest, athletic meet, etc.).

Name two golfers who, in your opinion, compete well.

Golfer #1: _____ **Golfer #2:** _____

List the characteristics, attributes, or behaviors that make them good competitors.

Golfer #1: _____ **Golfer #2:** _____

Golfer #1: _____ **Golfer #2:** _____

Golfer #1: _____ **Golfer #2:** _____

Is there anything on this list that the golfer cannot control?

_____

Recognizing this, what does this mean for you?

_____

Identify the top three characteristics, attributes, or behaviors from above that, if you improved, you would see the biggest results:

1. _____

2. _____

3. _____

What would happen or be different if you improved on the above things?

_____

Workout 5
Mental Point

Golfers put themselves in the best situation to be successful when they remember that winning is a by-product of their off-course preparation and on-course training which allows instincts to take over.

So You Want to Win!
What Will It Take?

What the Pros Are Saying

"I push myself to be the best I can be. I don't worry about what other people are doing, and I don't think about things I can't control."

—**Annika Sorenstam**, *Ten-time Major Champion*

"It's been fantastic to see the commitment with which Ernie [Els] has come in preparation for this event … in the last couple of years he's really put a lot of time and effort into it, leaving no stone unturned, so to speak."

—**Trevor Immelman**, *Masters champion and Assistant captain for Presidents Cup International Team*

"When I left my home for the United States, I was pretty sure I would never return and that I would die on the journey. But I wasn't going to die without a good fight. I've always kept that attitude, even today. I'm never going to stop fighting."

—**José de Jesús Rodríguez**, *Professional Golfer*

Key Principles

1. When you let go of expectations, you let go of what's out of your control.
2. The more emphasis that is placed on the outcome, the less time there is to concentrate on what's happening in the moment.
3. A key question to ask yourself: "How can I put myself in the best situation to be successful?"

So You Want to Win!

Tiger Woods once said, "I love to play golf and that's my arena. And you can characterize it and describe it however you want but I have a love and passion for getting that ball in the hole and beating those guys." Golfers and all athletes have one common trait; they all want to win! However, what separates a great golfer from a good golfer is the ability to focus on the specific steps they can control and let go of what they cannot. When a golfer's focus is consumed with the desire to only win they lose sight of the process, what they need to do for each round to be successful. Golf is unique and full of unknowns. Each course, hole, lie, and swing are completely different. There are never two shots that will be the same. If our mind is focused exclusively on the outcome there is very little opportunity to prepare mentally for what needs to happen in that specific moment during that specific shot. Jordan Spieth speaks to the importance of maintaining his focus on what he can control. He speaks about managing the situation, he is laser-focused on the present. "The hardest part is just managing the situation and managing the mental side. I knew physically that I could be there."

Golfers put themselves in the best situation to be successful when they remember that winning is a by-product of their off-course preparation and on-course training which allows their instincts to take over. Their attention should be harnessed around playing in the present moment with each swing of the club and not drifting on uncontrollable factors. Some uncontrollable factors might include letting your mind wander about previous results, what course you're playing, tee time, expectations of others and future holes or results to name a few.

Being present with each swing allows you to make necessary adjustments because you are keenly aware of what is needed for that specific shot. Your attention isn't divided between the past or future. You are solely focused on what is happening in the present moment. When you adapt and adjust on each shot the round will take care of itself. Certainly the game of golf is heavily based upon educated guesses, statistical probabilities, and understanding the layout of each course. Golfers must also embrace all of the unknown aspects of the game. When a golfer is completely present with each swing three things can happen:

- The golfer finds they are not good enough on that day to win.
- The golfer learns what skills need to be honed for the next tournament.
- The golfer exceeds their wildest expectations.

So You Want to Win!

We all want to win! However, most people don't realize that winning is often the result of specific actions. In other words, winning is a consequence. It doesn't happen on its own. Simply wanting to win is not good enough to be a great golfer.

It's important to understand and define what specific actions are necessary to begin the climb to put yourself in the best possible position to win.

On each line below list the actions that are necessary to prepare yourself to be in the best position to compete and give yourself the best opportunity to consistently play at your highest level.

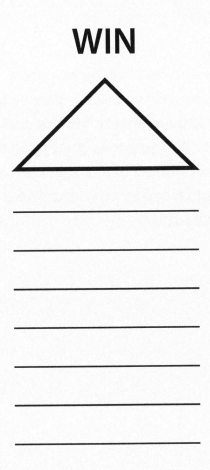

Workout 6

Mental Point

There are two kinds of goals: outcome and process. The outcome goal focuses solely on the end result. The process goal focuses on the individual steps a golfer needs to take in order to reach their outcome goal.

Goal Setting
Players Don't Plan to Fail, But They Do Fail to Plan

What the Pros Are Saying

"It's been a goal (#1 ranking) since I was 13, 14 years old…Seve is a very special player to all of us, and to be second to him, it's a true honor…it's a pretty unique feeling, so I'm going to enjoy it for a while."

—**Jon Rahm**, *Five-time PGA Tour winner*

"The best putters are confident with what they´re doing…when they walk onto a practice putting green they´re only concerned with their own feels and strokes…not concerned with what anyone else on that practice greens are doing…they´re comfortable with their own skin with what they´re doing."

—**Scotty Cameron**, *Master putter craftsman*

"The most important shot in golf is the next one."

—**Ben Hogan**, *Nine-time Major Champion*

Key Principles

1. Goals act as a compass, guiding you in a direction towards success.
2. Define success based on your individual process, not the outcome.
3. Focus on the process, what you can control, and your development.

Goal Setting

oal setting is a crucial aspect of the mental game when it comes to golf. If you were driving from New York to California, would you be able to do it without a GPS or even a map? The answer is no; as without proper directions, you would be all over the place. Chances are you would become lost and confused, never quite reaching your destination. Similar to a map, a golfer uses goals to keep "driving" forward and to help continual improvement. If you want to attain peak performance, setting goals and creating an approach to reach them is the ideal way to do it. Goals are a great tool to keep you committed and focused.

Goals should be challenging, individualized, and intrinsically motivated. Goals should be message-specific, so the golfer knows what they are trying to accomplish. Goals should also be time-specific, holding the golfer accountable for reaching what they are setting out for. Writing down the goals and keeping them in a place that the golfer can see daily are great ways to keep them at the top of the mind.

There are two kinds of goals: outcome and process. First, the outcome goal focuses solely on the end result. Secondly, the process goal focuses on the individual steps a golfer needs to take in order to reach their outcome goal. While an outcome goal may be to win a tournament, a process goal would ask, "What do I need to do to win? What steps must I take? How and when must I take them?" Outcome goals are out of the golfer's control, while the process goals focus on aspects of the game that the golfer can control. For example, a golfer cannot control the leaderboard of a tournament. However, they can control how much they prepare, how they warmed up, and how they approach each shot. Process-driven goals can include time spent on the range, workouts geared towards improving swing mechanics or working with a teaching pro to hone-in on the weak points of their game. Failure can even help lead to new goals! Eight-time PGA Tour winner and 2020 U.S. Open Champion Bryson DeChambeau, shared, "...if I get a bit in that hole, that's actually a good thing...I'll learn from it. Most people are afraid of failure. I love failure because it tells me where to go next."

An important aspect of goal setting is determining where the golfer currently is in regard to reaching their goal(s). A realistic and objective view will help the golfer become more aware of their situation. Goal setting will allow them to understand what they need to do and the appropriate steps to achieve their goals. Many golfers will only focus on result-oriented goals. This is a recipe for poor play. Arnold Palmer once said, "I have a tip that can take 5 strokes off anyone's golf game. It's called an eraser." Focusing on the process instead of the outcome will allow a golfer to play in the present and keep the focus on what they can control.

Both outcome and process-driven goals are important. I recommend that a player establish his outcome goals, and then determine the process goals to reach them. Tiger Woods is someone who decided not to get caught up in outcome goals. He once said, "The greatest thing about tomorrow is I will be better than I am today. And that's how I look at my life. I will be a better golfer…That's the beauty of tomorrow."

As Dr. Alan Goldberg, a noted mental training coach, says, "Once the competition starts, the outcome goal should be parked at the gate and the athlete should focus on the moment and the process of what they need to accomplish." Research has confirmed that reaching process-goals not only enhances performance but also reduces anxiety and builds a sense of confidence.

Focusing on the process…

Goal Setting

What is a goal you want to accomplish? _____
_____
_____

Why is this goal meaningful to you?
_____
_____

Rate, on a scale of 1–10, where you are now towards achieving this goal (10 = achieved goal).

What are three steps that you must do to achieve this goal?

1. _____

2. _____

3. _____

Do you have the skills to do these? If not, what skills are necessary to develop?
_____
_____

What can you do immediately to help you reach the goal?_____
_____
_____
_____

What can you do in the long term to reach this goal?

_____

_____

_____

In attempting to reach this goal, how hard do you think it will be?_____

_____

What could stop you?_____

Will you let it?_____

Workout 7
Mental Point

Golf's greats became that way by overcoming adversity, embracing challenges, and making the appropriate adjustments when the moment called for it on some of the biggest stages.

What Does it Take to Win?
Awareness and the 5 A's

What the Pros Are Saying

"I feel like I was really caring too much about the outcome and thinking about every little factor on every single shot…I had a lot of success early, but I feel like I was always trying to change something…I was trying to take a step forward and it honestly reversed my progress."

—**Matthew Wolff**, *One-time PGA Champion and Tour rookie*

"Forget the last shot. It takes so long to accept that you can't always replicate your swing. The only thing you can control is your attitude towards the next shot."

—**Mark McCumber**, *Players Champion*

"I got out of my element…It was so loud. And Tiger had shot a 64 and was making a charge, so it got even louder. Honestly, I wasn't even thinking about being in contention. I was thinking about playing with someone you've looked up to your whole life…Lesson #1? Don't ever do that again. It was the first time in my career that I lost focus on what I was doing." (2018 PGA Championship)

—**Gary Woodland**, *U.S. Open Champion*

Key Principles

1. Change starts with Awareness, Acknowledgment, Accountability, Adaptability, Adjustment, and Assessment.
2. Only through knowing where you are, can you get to where you want to be.
3. Setbacks provide a place for a fresh start.

What Does it Take to Win?

Who do you consider a hero? How about Captain Sullenberger? He was the U.S. Airways captain who safely landed Flight 1549 on the Hudson River and saved the lives of 155 passengers on January 15, 2009. Now think about legendary golfers, such as Arnold Palmer or Jack Nicklaus. These heroes and legends have common characteristics: courage, fearlessness, and calm under pressure, just to name a few. In order to be a hero or one of the sport's all-time greats, you must be able to manage adversity, embrace all challenges, and display the ability to adjust to each situation. One of today's greats, Phil Mickelson was quoted as saying, "The thing I was proud of about today's round was that on this course, everybody is going to make mistakes, but sometimes it's hard to forget about it and let it go. After I made a double on 1, I was able to be patient and let it go and came back with birdies on 3 and 5. When I bogeyed 6, I was able to let it go and come back with a birdie on 8. I was able to let go of some bad shots and forget about it and move on." Phil knew the importance of being able to bounce back and adjust. He knew about needing to be calm under stress and embracing adversity in pressure-packed situations.

We often get mesmerized by the winners, lauding them as superheroes. Yet, the most important component is "what it took" to make victory possible. How do they compete so hard, effectively, and consistently? Golf's greats became that way by overcoming adversity, embracing challenges, and making the appropriate adjustments when the moment called for it on some of the biggest stages. There is a saying, "You can't change the wind, but you can change the direction of the sails."

We have all seen golfers repeatedly do the same thing, leading to the same results. Think about the golfers who refuse to make adjustments to their game—whether it is trying to attack difficult pin placements, or not adjusting to the speed of the greens. You will see these golfers play too risky or make the same errors in judgment and never see improvement. Einstein once said, "The definition of insanity is doing the same thing over and over and expecting different results."

Probably the most important component of golf, and life, is the ability to be aware of a situation and adjust to it. Golfers need to be great problem-solvers. In order to do this, it's imperative to have a framework in place that you are able to systematically apply. The remainder of this workout will focus on this framework, and what I believe to be the most essential mental characteristics for improvement, success, and ultimately reaching your personal peak performance as a golfer. This framework includes Awareness and the five A's: Acknowledgment, Accountability, Adjustability, Adaptability, and Assessment. Without this framework, a golfer will be unaware of the present moment, and consequently unable to make the proper adjustments needed to succeed.

Awareness

The first step in solving any problem is having awareness—without being aware, a golfer is unable to assess and determine the current reality of a situation. Awareness entails simply and non-judgmentally observing what is happening. In different situations, this is especially critical as momentum and circumstances can shift dramatically on one hole. Remaining in the present allows you to accurately assess a situation, adjust, and position yourself accordingly. If you find yourself stuck on a previous shot, or even a previous hole or tournament, your perception of the situation on the current shot will be skewed. Similarly, if you are focused on the future, you will be unable to accurately see what is unfolding in front of you.

Acknowledgment

By acknowledging a situation, you do not necessarily have to like it. If you are down by a stroke going into the final hole of a tournament, you can acknowledge what is happening and then decide what you can do about it and how to approach the situation. This will help ensure success! Golfers may often say, "Why should I acknowledge it? That implies complacency." This

is not so. Acknowledgment simply means that you are aware of the current reality of the situation. In effect, I am suggesting that this provides a choice and the opportunity to either make the change or do nothing.

Accountability

If a golfer does not take accountability, they will blame the circumstances on something else, like the weather or crowd noise, and nothing will change. This attribute can be painful but refer to this saying, "It may hurt, but the truth will set you free." Take Justin Thomas for example, he said, "It's completely unacceptable to give up a three-shot lead with three to go. I'm upset, I'm disappointed in myself, but at the end of the day it's over with now, and I just need to take some time this afternoon and tonight to build on it and figure out what I can do better going into next week." He took responsibility for his poor play and set forth a plan of action to be better. It is normal to have a bad round, and it is imperative that you take ownership of your mistakes, be accountable, and then learn and build off each and every one of them.

Adaptability

This refers to adapting internally and responding to the situation during a tournament that puts you in position to be able to perform at your best—in other words, being able to mentally reframe a situation. Once a golfer can go from the negative to the neutral (or, preferably, the positive), they can change the situation towards their advantage. Internal adaptation is imperative. Without this, the actions will have no power, passion, or meaning. More often than not, a golfer will need to change their mindset, and emotional perspective, rather than their strategy, to earn success.

Adjustability

This refers to making changes in physical or technical strategy, based on the situation. Jim Furyk, when describing having to play Augusta National, said, "There's going to be places where you can attack the golf course and there's going to be times where you've got to kind of bite your lip and play conservative and hit certain spots on the green, get out of there with a par and move on." Each course, each hole, and each lie will be different, which means knowing how to adjust to every shot will make a huge difference in your game.

Assessment

This is continual and must be done after a golfer has made their adjustments and adapted. Oftentimes, a golfer is very close to achieving their goal, but they just need to settle in. Other times, another small tweak may be needed to succeed. Without the assessment, it is not possible to determine the results of the previous steps. Additionally, this step allows the entire process to officially be en route to achieving your goal.

Awareness and the 5 A's is a formula to problem solving on the course and in life. This formula can be seen being used by some of the greatest to ever swing a club from all-time greats like Nicklaus, Player, and Palmer, to great golfers today like Woods, Mickelson, and McIlroy. Think about what it takes to accomplish anything significant in life. Inevitably, awareness and the 5 A's will be necessary, whether it be taking a test, or winning the Masters. Remember, you can't be your best unless you overcome adversity. The only way is to be aware of it, acknowledge it, be accountable, internally adapt to it, externally make the required adjustments, and then assess what needs to be done and get ready to start progressing and developing into the player you were meant to be!

What Does it Take to Win?

The solution to any problem starts with awareness!

Awareness: Name a specific golf shot or situation that is troubling you. (describe it) _____

Acknowledgment: What can you do to acknowledge the situation?

_____

Accountability: What can you do to take accountability for the situation?

_____

Adjustability: What can you do to physically adjust to change the situation?

_____

Adaptability: What can you do to mentally adapt to change the situation?

_____

Assessment: Based on the previous steps, how would you assess things?

_____

Workout 8
Mental Point

As athletes, we are all capable of playing inside the zone. It is a natural state that is experienced rather than invented. It is not a destination that you travel to; rather it is a place that when you let go of all the distractions within and stay present, it will find you.

Golf Inside the Zone
One Stroke at a Time

What the Pros Are Saying

"I try to feel oily…When I swing at a golf ball right, my mind is blank and my body is loose as a goose."

—**Sam Snead**, *Seven-time Major Champion*

"For me the U.S. Open at Oakmont in 2016 was probably the most focused I've been from start to finish in a golf tournament. Thinking correctly, making the right decisions—It sounds easy to focus for the whole time, for four rounds, but to focus on every shot for one day, it's difficult."

—**Dustin Johnson**, *Two-time Major Champion*

"It should be the shot that makes the swing, not the swing that makes the shot."

—**David Mackenzie**, *Mental Coach*

Key Principles

1. Try softer, not harder.
2. Trust yourself—the real answers are inside.
3. Remember your training—trust your instincts.

Golf Inside the Zone

The "zone" is a state of being entirely in the present, one that exists within each of us and free of all distractions. Golf inside the zone requires a golfer to have awareness, to not over-think, over-judge, or over-try. Inside the zone requires an implicit acceptance of what the golfer is experiencing at any particular time. It will build a state where the golfer no longer analyzes technique but just competes. The result is usually a smooth, harmonious, effortless, flow of energy that produces an unencumbered swing.

These moments were also defined as "peak experiences" by the humanistic psychologist Dr. Abraham Maslow. His research indicated that those who achieved such "peak experiences" felt: 'more integrated;' 'at one with the experience;' 'relatively egoless;' 'fully functioning;' 'in the groove;' 'free of blocks, inhibitions, cautions, fears, doubts, controls, reservations, and self-criticism;' 'spontaneous and more creative;' 'in the here and now.' To sum it all up: the feat being attempted is effortless, like flowing water.

As athletes, we are all capable of playing inside the zone. It is a natural state that is experienced rather than invented. It is not a destination that you travel to; rather it is a place that when you let go of all the distractions within and stay present, it will find you. This feeling is aptly addressed in the 2000 movie "The Legend of Bagger Vance," starring Will Smith as the caddie Bagger Vance and Matt Damon as the famous golfer, Rudolf Junuh. Vance says to Junuh: "Inside each and every one of us is one true authentic swing…Somethin' we was born with…Somethin' that's ours and ours alone…Somethin' that can't be taught to ya or learned…Somethin' that's got to be remembered…Over time the world can rob us of that swing…It can get buried inside us under all our wouldas and couldas and shouldas…Some folk even forget what their swing was like…Close your eyes…Feel the ball…"

Golf inside the zone is innate in every person; in fact, each of us has already experienced this seemingly unattainable state as a young child. Born into this world, the unassuming child breathes deeply and instinctively through his or her nose. We learn best when we are young, free from stress, and outside distractions that pull us away from the present moment. Taking your first steps as a child requires trust-in-self, determination, and trial-and-error. Most children learn to walk before their parents actually teach them. They learn through observation, natural instinct, and modeling others around them. Through this process of learning to walk, one gains confidence in the natural and instinctual learning process that operates within them. Conversely, parents watch their children's efforts with love and interest, but usually without much interference. When a child loses his or her balance and falls, the mother does not condemn the child as clumsy or uncoordinated; she doesn't even feel bad about the tumble. She simply notices the event and provides a kind word, support, and usually a loving gesture of encouragement. Consequently, a child's progress in learning to walk is never hindered by the idea that he or she is not doing better. If we could only treat our teenage and adult athletic endeavors, such as in golf, as we do a child learning to walk, we would make tremendous progress toward uninhibited and non-comparative improvement—the stepping stone to effortless peak performance.

Michelangelo, the infamous Italian sculptor, provides a classic metaphor of focusing on the process and getting inside the zone. He sculpted the Renaissance masterpiece, David, from 1501 to 1504. Undeterred by the challenging tasks of carving a statue out of a mere slab of marble, Michelangelo had a vision of the finished product; he worked under the premise that the image of David was already in the block of stone, a concept referred to as disegno. He chipped away at the stone and brought out what others could not even imagine. He saw and knew what others did not. The marble he was chipping away was a metaphor for the distractions, limitations, fears, anxieties, negative self-talk, and uncontrollable events that get in most people's way. Michelangelo knew David existed, but he had to let him appear. Similarly, our best performances are waiting to happen once we let go of distractions, fear of failure, and our ego.

It can be challenging to golf in the present. However, by focusing on your breath, the present situation, and your pre-shot routine, the zone can be achieved. While it is helpful to learn from the past and set goals to achieve in the future, it is imperative that a golfer lets go of such thoughts and just competes in the present moment. Remember what Hall of Fame golfer, Tommy Bolt, once said, "The mind messes up more shots than the body."

The gift of the body is that it is always centered and present. To move into the part of you that has the power to transform your life experiences and perform without limits, you must bring your awareness to your body, your breath, your senses, and start from the inside out; much like the eye of a hurricane: still on the inside and unpredictable on the outside. Bagger Vance knew this. He said, "There's only one shot that's in perfect harmony with the field…One shot that's his authentic shot…there's a perfect shot out there tryin' to find each of us…All we got to do is get ourselves out of its way, to let it choose us…Seek it with your hands. Don't think about it…Feel it."

Golf Inside the Zone

Remember a time…when everything was flowing and you were playing golf inside the zone.

When was it? _____

What time was it? _____

Where was it? _____

How old were you? _____

What were you wearing? _____

What was the weather? _____

Who was watching? _____

What did it feel like? _____

_____

What smells did you notice? _____

What was happening? _____

_____

What sounds did you notice? _____

_____

What was your sense of time? _____

What was going through your head? _____

_____

Overall, what words or images come to mind? _____

_____

What else do you remember about that time you were playing Inside the Zone?

_____

_____

_____

Connecting to your 'Inside the Zone' image is similar to how the top golf pros use their pre-shot routine to help them let go and relax before hitting the next shot.

How can you use your 'Inside the Zone' image to help you?_____

_____

_____

_____

_____

_____

_____

Workout 9
Mental Point

When a golfer uses imagery, they are creating a blueprint of the shot.

Mental Imagery!
How Imagery Can Help You Win

What the Pros Are Saying

"I never hit a shot, not even in practice, without having a very sharp, in-focus picture of it in my head."

—**Jack Nicklaus**, *Eighteen-time Major Champion*

"Visualization is the most powerful thing we have."

—**Sir Nick Faldo**, *Six-time Major Champion*

"Watching that video of me winning the U.S. Open, that helped me to believe that my putting was good enough, that my ball-striking was good enough, even though it's a few years back. But it's always nice to remember those moments and feel the same that you felt that day."

—**Martin Kaymer**, *Two-time Major Champion*

Key Principles

1. Feel it, see it…do it!
2. If you can see it, you can do it.

Mental Imagery!

What images come to mind when you hear phrases such as "imagine if..." or "remember a time...?" For most, these words start a flashback to certain situations or moments on or off the course. Can you remember a time when you striped a drive and positioned yourself for the perfect angle for your approach shot? If you are truly in-tune with yourself you might also hear the click of the ball flying off the club and you can see the trajectory of the ball in the sky. The concept of visualization is to create a mental picture of a situation before it happens.

This workout will highlight different aspects of imagery: What is imagery? Who is using it? When can it be used? How can it be used? And how can it help improve your performance on the course?

I use imagery as a key mental skill with the golfers I work with. The most important component when beginning to use imagery is that the golfer is relaxed, centered and calm. Before we start we usually take a few breaths.

What is imagery? Imagery is the purposeful act of rehearsing a task mentally with the intent of learning it. When a golfer uses imagery, they are creating a blueprint of the shot. It incorporates all of the senses: visual, kinesthetic, auditory, tactile, and olfactory. Additionally, it involves imagination, emotion, feelings, and moods. Essentially, the idea is to use your imagination to create or recreate a situation in the future, which will help you prepare for any possible scenario. While being up a stroke on the final hole with the only thing between you and winning is a six-foot putt to seal the tournament; a golfer may visualize the break the ball must take in order to sink the putt.

Who uses imagery? All top athletes and golfers do. I suspect you have even used it—it is almost impossible not to have done so at some point. Have you ever imagined receiving a present or eating your favorite food or going out with a friend? Have you ever studied for a test where you ran scenarios through your mind, planning out the best way to solve a problem? Most people use imagery in their day-to-day life without even knowing it. Imagine what would happen if you incorporated it into your day-to-day golf practices with intention? If you are like most golfers, it will be beneficial.

When can imagery be used? Imagery can be used to practice certain shots, mechanical adjustments, routines, or situations that golfers are trying to incorporate into their game. Maybe you want to learn a different technique that allows you to gain yardage off the tee or introduce a new stance to improve your impact position. It can also be used to prepare for the unexpected situation that is likely to present itself during a tournament. Maybe this includes being in contention on the Sunday back nine at the Masters? Tiger Woods won his 5th green jacket in 2019 after overcoming major injuries that plagued his game for years. He said, "This one feels special in its own way…This year, to go 14 years between jackets is a long time…And on top of that to actually have won my first major championship coming from behind. It's so ironic given my last few years of what I've kind of had to battle through, that now is finally the time I finally come from behind when I've had more game throughout the years, and I've had more runs, and I've been in situations where I've been in better spots…For some reason I got it done." Woods is said to use imagery—certainly it may have prepared Tiger to come out and play with confidence.

How can imagery be used? Picture a golfer's game that you admire and would like to model. Specifically, identify the characteristics and attributes of that golfer that make them unique and what you, as a golfer, would look like with these attributes. For instance, take Greg Norman's ability to drive the ball straight and far, or Jack Nicklaus's clutch putting. Visualize yourself playing with the skills you believe make a great golfer. You will become empowered as you see yourself playing with skill and confidence.

Golfers can also imagine specific difficult situations such as a plugged greenside bunker lie. By imagining the feelings and emotions of facing that lie, the golfer then imagines making the proper adjustments in their stance and grip for a positive outcome to occur.

How will getting comfortable using imagery help you improve your performance? It's easy! Practice imagery for five-minutes a day. The body's central nervous system doesn't differentiate between the actual event or imagery, therefore practicing imagery on its own will be helpful. Even better, for example, visualize the line and break of the ball on a putt and then hit it. This programs your system to already have experienced the emotions of that putt dropping. Soon enough you will become more comfortable with the skill or situation.

Mental Imagery!

Self-Guided Imagery Script (instructions: read the script slowly, and notice what you experience as you read the words)

Find a comfortable position…just be aware of the sounds around you, just taking them in…Notice your breathing…and just observe its natural rhythm…No need to judge yourself, your thoughts or your feelings…just notice them for the moment…let them float by…allowing yourself this moment of quiet…You may begin to notice your body slowing down…feeling your body unwind…just let it unfold…observe this natural pendulum…

Now, would it be okay to turn your attention inward…I wonder if you can take yourself to a special place…a place you feel comfortable and secure…a place we will call Inside Your Zone…in this place…you're relaxed…it can be a place you have visited before…or a place you can only can go via your imagination…or it can be a place in your body, or even a feeling somewhere deep inside…that brings comfort…peace…it can be a combination of all these things…or anything…know one thing…this is your zone…and no one else's…As you look around…notice the surroundings…notice the smell…notice the feel…let it unfold…notice the sounds…sights…smells…or even tastes…

With this feeling of being inside your zone…shift your attention to the fairway or green…just notice what you see…let it unfold…in front of you…bring your awareness to a time you played great…a time you did your best…be aware of the experience…feel it unfold…notice your energy…and your confidence…from inside YOUR zone…

What's it like to do your best…put it all on the line…play from your heart…would it be okay to stay with this feeling…even make some space for it…just notice what happens…

Now, gently bring attention back to your breathing…know you can go back to YOUR zone…any time you want…keep in mind you have the super player inside…you have the energy inside…use it…tap into it…

When you are ready…slowly bring yourself back…be aware of what your feet feel like touching the floor…notice the sounds around you…gently open your eyes…

How do you feel now?_____

_____

_____

_____

Look out into the ocean…Simply observe your breath…Notice what you experience in your body…When you're nervous during a round, it can be helpful (between shots) to bring up a time when you were calm.

*Bonding —
as only
golfers do…*

Section 2
PRE-ROUND WORKOUTS

Pre-Round Workouts

Can you remember a time you wanted to do something?
But, you were scared to "just let go" and "go for it?"

Imagine this… life is an ocean and you're a surfer.
At first you're afraid to get into the water.

Finally you go in and begin to trust the ocean.
Wading further out, going with the flow…

You realize, when you allow,
It starts to get easier; the water carries you.

Once you become comfortable with the ocean,
You look ahead; decide which waves to ride.
Steering away from trouble, rocks and other surfers.
Choosing the best way
While still going with the flow…

—**Rob Polishook**, *author of* Golf Inside the Zone

Workout 10
Mental Point

Nervousness is not bad, nervousness is not good. Nervousness just is...Accept it and it usually dissolves away...

OMG!...I'm Nervous!
Five Ways to Work Through Pre-Round Jitters

What the Pros Are Saying

"If I wasn't nervous, that would mean I didn't care. I don't want to be out there flat. I want to be out here so bad. And now I am."

—**Tiger Woods**, *Fifteen-time Major Champion*

"To play well you must feel tranquil and at peace. I have never been troubled by nerves in golf because I felt I had nothing to lose and everything to gain."

—**Harry Vardon**, *Seven-time Major Champion*

"Being nervous is not something you should be ashamed of. Nervous means you care, you really want to do well."

—**Paula Creamer**, *One-time Major Champion*

Key Principles

1. Everyone gets nervous.

2. If you're not nervous, you're not human.

3. Nerves are a great indicator of passion!

OMG!...I'm Nervous!

Buzz, Buzz. It's usually a weekend, in my world. I may have just finished watching a morning segment on ESPN or caught a group teeing off in whatever tournament may be on that weekend. All is relaxed while I drink my morning coffee. Yet, for the golfer on the other end of my buzzing cell phone, their world could be anything but calm. Butterflies are fluttering in their stomach. Their head may be spinning with possible performance outcomes and self-doubt could be creeping in.

The golfer wonders what is happening to them. Perhaps this golfer, whose strength is their short game, is facing a course requiring long-approach shots or a golfer who's struggling with his lag putting has to face a course with severe undulating greens. It is at this very moment our paths connect with that Buzz on the cell phone or a short but direct text message. It is always the same: I hear or read, "I'm nervous—what can I do?"

As a mental training coach, this is probably the most commonly asked question I receive. As many golfers who have experienced such jitters can attest it's usually not the nervousness itself that presents the problem but all the thoughts that accompany it. For example, "Why am I nervous?" or "What happens if I'm still this nervous as I tee it up on the first hole?" This then sets off another negative spiral and the golfer's natural nervousness turns into a far more debilitating anxiety.

In light of this, I want to share five ideas with which the nervous golfer can gain some perspective over what's happening and be able to better manage and work through excessive nervousness.

1. It's okay to be nervous.

It's perfectly normal and natural. In fact, even some of the top golfers in the world admit nervousness is a problem. One time Major Champion, Keegan Bradley, has been battling nervousness for some time now. "If I feel nervous, I just feel it, try to accept it, and move on. I don't try and block it out." Bradley has learned to embrace his nerves and play through them. Being able to accept your nerves is actually the best way to manage the situation. The top golfers don't fight the tension; rather they accept it, as "something inside of them is nervous." How many of you have tried to resist a feeling or thought? What happens? It usually gets more intense and continues to loom in the back of your mind.

2. Nervousness is a sign that you care. Nervousness isn't bad, nervousness isn't good.

It simply exists. It's your own unique way of reacting to different situations throughout a tournament or round. Going back to Keegan Bradley's story, he too had learned that his nerves showcased his effort. "When you feel nerves, it's a good thing," he said. "It means you are doing something right. Especially in a Major." Bradley has learned that his nerves exist simply because he cared enough about his performance. Nerves meant he "was doing something right." There are always going to be two sides to everything, but when you are nervous, usually you only focus on the negative aspects of how you feel. Think about it, as a golfer, you can feel anxious anytime you approach the ball. The anxiousness builds, the round begins to speed up, and you grip the club a little tighter. However, what is the other side? Aren't you also excited, challenged, aware, and maybe even focused because you have a great opportunity in front of you? You're contending late in a round that you've imagined yourself being in since you were a little kid playing miniature golf. Remember: embrace this challenge. Your nerves are simply a by-product of the thrill.

3. If you are nervous, so are your opponents.

When a golfer is nervous, their focus is usually entirely on themselves and they are not seeing the entire picture. They are merely seeing a small piece of it. Do not forget about your opponents! The other golfers in the field account for the rest of the puzzle. In fact, that golfer you are paired with is just as nervous as you are; perhaps even more so!

4. What's the worst that can happen?

When Tiger Woods was returning to golf, in 2016, he was nervous about coming back. "Yes, I'm nervous," Woods said "I'm nervous for every tournament I play in, whether it's after a layoff, or six in a row, or a Major. If I care, I'm nervous and it's good to be that way. To have that nervous energy and channel it into aggression, into focus, into concentration, that's the good stuff." So, what's the worst that can happen? By accepting and feeding into that nervous energy, you can truly unleash your best self. Like Tiger said, take it, channel it, and use it *for* you instead of *against* you.

5. Why am I nervous?

When I ask that question to golfers, they usually say it's because "I want to win," or "I don't know how I'm going to do." What is important to understand is that the golfer's focus is distracted. Their focus is on something they cannot control which is winning (the result). More so, they are focusing on another uncontrollable, which is their opponent. Sometimes, a golfer might focus in on how an opponent might be hitting at the range or on the putting green prior to a tournament. Once you focus on the uncontrollable, there is little time to focus on what you can control and what one needs to do to perform their best.

The next time you are nervous, refer to the five ideas mentioned in this chapter to help you shift your focus and play your best round!

OMG!...I'm Nervous!

What's important to understand with nerves is that everyone gets nervous. In fact, if you're not nervous, you're probably not human! Two reasons you're nervous are that you care and that you want to do well. Certainly understandable! Further, if you're nervous...I bet your opponents are also. So...maybe it's okay to be nervous!

Remember a round where you were nervous, but everything worked out great in the end. Describe it.

_____

_____

_____

_____

What were you feeling? _____

_____

_____

What did you notice about the nerves as the round went on? _____

_____

_____

What would your experience be if you didn't judge the nervousness as good or bad? _____

_____

_____

Using the principles from this chapter, what could you say to yourself to manage the nervousness? _____

_____

_____

_____

_____

How could you reframe your nerves in a way that could help you?_____

1. _____

2. _____

3. _____

How would doing the above help you in tense situations? _____

The ABCs of the mental game: Accept. Breathe. Concentrate.

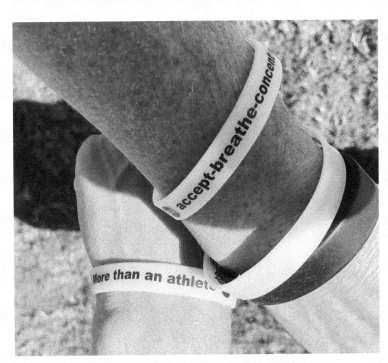

Workout 11
Mental Point

Bring your attention to your breath. For a moment... simply notice the sound of your breath, then notice the feel of your breath, then notice the rhythm of your breath. Just be curious...

How to Play in the Moment
It's as Easy as Breathing

What the Pros Are Saying

"Golf is all about the present tense... If you're in the future tense, whether it's thinking about what it would be like to be a winner, thinking ahead about what you're going to do with the winner's check, or thinking about how bad it would be to blow the tournament, you're not in the moment."

—**Peter Kostis**, *PGA Tour swing coach*

"You always have to fit your game to the golf course, so that's the fun of it, learning how to do that."

—**Jack Nicklaus**, *Eighteen-time Major Champion*

"Once you address the golf ball, hitting it has to be the most important thing in your life at that moment. Shut out all thoughts other than picking out a target and take dead aim at it. That is a good way to calm a case of the nerves."

—**Harvey Penick**, *Legendary Texas golf coach and teacher*

Key Principles

1. Your breath is always in the present moment.

2. Focus on your breath—calm on the inside, aware on the outside.

3. Notice your breath and let go of everything else.

How to Play in the Moment

While you're reading this workout you are breathing. The majority of us take this subtle automatic action for granted. Why is this? Breathing is regulated by our autonomic nervous system so we breathe without our conscious awareness. By bringing your awareness to your breath it will calm you, slow you down, and help you reach that present state of mind where you are focused, centered, and relaxed.

Our mind can drift into two places: the past and the future. When our mind is focused on the past, we are usually conjuring up thoughts, feelings, and images of memories that have stayed with us. Examples of this might include a poorly struck shot that didn't carry over the water or a 2-foot birdie putt that just lipped out.

When our mind drifts into the future, we are usually focused on expectations of what we hope is going to happen. While on the tee, you may be thinking "if I just par the last three holes I will beat my low score." How many of us have let our minds drift away from the present and have gone on a bogey train? To focus on either the past or future leads to mental errors! Both fall into the realm of what a golfer cannot control. Golfers can only control the present by preparing for their next shot and that is where their focus must remain.

Fortunately, our body and breath are always in the present. It is said that the *present* is named as such because being in the present is literally a gift! Our breath is one of the greatest gifts of all. When this tool is used properly it can serve as an anchor helping us to stay centered and focused. Simply bringing our attention to the natural rhythm of our breath can take our focus away from stressful situations and connect us to our body, rhythm, and natural timing.

Try this experiment: Ask yourself, "Am I breathing?" Sit silently for 30 seconds and notice what happens. Usually, you will find yourself becoming more aware and slowing down. The following three breathing practices can be used to guide you to stay centered, focused, and in a state of calm awareness. Practice them off the course. Then, use the one that feels best for you between shots, holes, or anytime you feel yourself losing focus.

1. Unguided Breathing

The object here is to bring your attention to your natural breathing, wherever it is, at the present moment. Just be aware of one of the following senses: sound, feel, or rhythm. How does your breath sound? How does it feel? Notice its rhythm at that moment. Do not try to change anything or judge it. Just observe its natural organic pace. You may even prompt yourself by asking, "Am I breathing?" What you will usually notice after five or ten seconds is that your breath will slow down, and so will the pace of the round.

2. Word Association Breathing

As you breathe in, say to yourself the word relaxation, slow, or patient and imagine what it would feel like to feel each of those. Then exhale, and say the word anxious or fast, and imagine what it would feel like to let go of the anxiousness on the tee, green, or anywhere in-between. Visualize tension leaving your body and feel your internal clock at just the right speed. You may make up your own words to suit your situation. However, the key is to inhale what you want, and exhale what you do not need.

3. Rhythmic Breathing

The object here is to breathe to an established rhythm that feels best for you. What's important with this exercise is that you find a pattern that works for you and stick to it. Try inhaling to the count of three, hold your breath for two counts, and then exhale to the count of four. When a golfer is *on* and they just do not seem to miss their shots, we say they've found a rhythm. The idea here is for you to find your rhythm using your breath! What

feels best? Be creative and experiment with your own rhythms. Have fun with it!

Whichever breathing practice you choose, once you are centered with a soft focus on your breath, allow your eyes to wander and your attention to expand and take everything in around you. Be aware of sights and thoughts as they pass by. Metaphorically, this breathing practice is similar to the eye of the hurricane; you are calm on the inside but very active on the outside. Bubba Watson shared his thoughts when discussing his new breathing techniques prior to shooting a 65 at Riviera, "Off the course, I'm even-keeled. I can kind of relax, but on course is where I get headless and I start going, ramped up, going too fast, and so we are trying to slow down to where I am off the course and so that's what we are working on, trying to do that. And then finally I guess as I get older, I get smarter, I realize maybe I should work on it. I work on putting and chipping. Maybe I can work on the mental part."

Slowing down a round with your breath allows you to respond to each swing, hole, round, or tournament with clarity. Remember: clarity creates consistency, and consistency is the name of the game!

How to Play in the Moment

It's as Easy as Breathing!

Breathing is regulated by our autonomic nervous system: It happens without thinking (fortunately!). By bringing attention to our breath, it helps connect us to our ever-present body.

Below are three different breathing exercises that can be used prior to any shot, or anytime you need to slow down, change your focus, and calm down.

Unguided Breathing Exercise

Start this exercise by asking yourself... Am I breathing? Then, simply notice your natural in and out breaths. One breath at a time, notice the sound, feel, and then rhythm—whichever sense you connect best with. Just be aware of that and be curious. Notice how you may let go of everything else as you do this.

Word Association Breathing Exercise

List characteristics, attributes, or emotions you would want to breathe in and breathe out.

Breathe in: *patience* _____ **Breathe out:** *fear* _____

Breathe in: _____ **Breathe out:** _____

Breathe in: _____ **Breathe out:** _____

Now, as you breathe in, imagine what it would feel like to breathe patience in, to feel patience flowing through. Then imagine what it would look like to breathe fear out, and visualize the fear dissipating like a cloud in the wind. Do the same thing with the words that feel right for you.

Rhythmic Breathing Exercise

Breathe in and count how many seconds the breath is…Then, notice a possible pause, then breathe out and notice how many seconds it is. Discover your rhythm. What feels best?

Beats in: _____ **Beats holding breath:** _____ **Beats out:** _____

Summary

These three breathing exercises are intended to help athletes slow down, change focus, and stay in the present. Experiment with each exercise to discover which ones you can incorporate into your off-course, pre, mid, and post round routines.

Workout 12
Mental Point

Remember to tune into your internal MPS when you are on the course. Be aware and objectively assess your positioning on each hole.

Course Management
Playing With Your Mental Positioning System

What the Pros Are Saying

"Be decisive. A wrong decision is generally less disastrous than indecision."

—**Bernhard Langer**, *Two-time Masters Champion*
and eleven-time Senior Tour Major Champion

"It's very satisfying knowing, like, I'm not near as long as some of these guys and I'm able to kind of use my skills of distance control and shot shape to kind of pick me back up when I'm 40 yards or 30 yards behind these guys."

—**Webb Simpson**, *U.S. Open and Players Champion*

"For true success, it matters what our goals are. And it matters how we go about attaining them. The means are as important as the ends. How we get there is as important as where we go."

—**Old Tom Morris**, *Four-time Open Champion*

Key Principles

1. Change starts with awareness.
2. You are where you are…Stay in the moment.
3. Trust your process.

Course Management

Let's flash back a few years to a time when people read maps to determine how to reach a destination. Three steps were necessary: first, you needed to be aware of your current location; second, you needed to know where you wanted to go; and third, you needed to plan the most efficient route to reach your desired destination.

In today's day and age, map reading has been replaced with access to global positioning systems (GPS) in our cell phones or cars. Certainly, the GPS application has made it easier to reach your destination than ever before. All that is necessary is to input the destination and et voilá—the GPS tells you exactly where to go and how to get there. There need be little awareness of where you currently are and no thinking or planning is required. So, what does this have to do with golf? Everything…stay with me.

On the golf course, we cannot turn to our GPS to reach our goals. Thankfully, all golfers have a similar yet superior tool called cognition. This tool is what I refer to as the MPS, or Mental Positioning System. The MPS is a human machine run by the strongest computer in the universe; not an electric device but our own brain. MPS is activated by awareness. It requires us to examine the same three key points we needed to ask when using a map: where we are at this exact point in time, where do we want to end up, and what the necessary steps are in order to reach that goal.

Fortunately, a golfer can employ their MPS in both practice and tournaments. Once aware, the golfer's MPS can tell them where they are in a particular situation and what adjustments or steps need to be taken.

Some golfers may use their MPS more than others and consequently reap the benefits while others may take the shortcuts that our GPS uses. For example, many golfers simply say, "I want to win"—in other words they input their GPS destination without any awareness to what is necessary to win. Your MPS empowers you to walk your unique path without short cuts. Though using the MPS may take longer because it's the only path to improvement, growth, and consistency. Hall of Fame golfer, "Old Tom Morris," once said, "For true success, it matters what our goals are. And it matters how we go about attaining them. The means are as important as the ends. How we get there is as important as where we go." Taking the shorter GPS route often will end with an inconsistent approach and performances on the course.

During a tournament, it is imperative to be aware and realize that each situation changes stroke-by-stroke. Furthermore, it is key to understand tendencies and patterns of your game and the various courses you will play.

To use your MPS properly in practice ask yourself these questions:

- Where am I now, with regard to a particular skill?
- Where do I want to be in a certain amount of time?
- To get there, what do I have to do/ what will it take?
- Am I willing to put in the effort to do this? Who can help me?
- How will I know when I reach this goal?

To use your MPS during your round ask yourself these questions:

- What is happening at this moment?
- What do I want to happen?
- What adjustments do I need to make?
- How would the situation change if I made these adjustments?
- What's one adjustment I can make now?

Remember to tune into your internal MPS. Be aware and objectively assess your positioning on each hole. This will help you to make the best possible choices and decisions while playing. You will find that using your MPS for course corrections is not only empowering, but will help you adapt and adjust during your round.

Course Management

You can't get somewhere without being aware of knowing where you are! Try completing the following three steps in regard to a goal or challenge.

Describe where you currently are in regard to a goal or challenge. This is similar to your GPS recognizing where you are. _____

_____

_____

_____

_____

Describe where you want to be in regard to a goal or challenge. This is similar to entering your destination address. _____

_____

_____

_____

_____

Knowing where you are now and where you want to be . . . what three things do you need to do to get there? This is similar to the GPS displaying the route.

1. _____

2 _____

3. _____

Workout 13
Mental Point

As a golfer it is important to take ownership of your time during practice. Utilize it as a means of putting yourself in varying situations and lies that you may face during a tournament.

Why Can't I Play Rounds Like I Practice?
Five Reasons This Happens

What the Pros Are Saying

"I think block practice is ok up to a certain point…I'm a huge advocate of getting on the golf course as much as you can. You can hit balls all day long on the range, but you have to do it on the course. Once on the course, you can forget about the range…just think about hitting shots on the course."

—**Brandel Chamblee**, *Former PGA Tour Pro and lead analyst on the Golf Channel*

"Being 10 years (having never won a professional tournament) I definitely had some scar tissue…If you're not nervous, you're not alive…I definitely had some nerves going…but I think I knew in my own mind that I was going to get it done, it was just a matter of time of me getting out of my own way and letting it happen."

—**Jason Kokrak**, *One-time PGA tour winner*

"Of all the hazards, fear is the worst."

—**Sam Snead**, *Nine-time Major Champion*

Key Principles

1. A round is different than practice.
2. The more you need to win, the less you will.
3. Practice the process.

Why Can't I Play Rounds Like I Practice?

"**W**hy can't I take my practice game to the course?" It's probably the second most asked question I hear from golfers; exceeded only by some variation of "I'm nervous, what do I do?" Sometimes this question comes out as a defiant statement where the golfer stubbornly says, "If I hit the ball off the tee like I was hitting on the range, I would have put myself in better positions throughout the tournament." Interestingly, that statement is usually true. Yet, practice and tournaments are different from each other in both intensity and pressure.

In practice, whether at the driving range, putting green or even just playing a round for fun, we are usually competing against ourselves to improve our own game. However, when we compete in a tournament there are added components which serve to distract us. For example, your opponents. What would happen if you thought of them as as partners? Yes, not your enemy. They are there to force you to improve, to make you uncomfortable, and help you learn from adversity.

Three time Major Champion, Jordan Spieth, said, "I feel like you can look at it a couple of ways. You can get really upset and complain about it, which I've done, and that's not helpful, or you can look at it like, hey, this is part of the game testing you, and the better you handle these situations, the faster you progress forward."

The remainder of this workout will explore five key reasons why golfers perform differently in practice and during competition.

1. Loss of Focus

Throughout a tournament, a golfer's focus is usually on the outcome rather than the present moment. When a golfer focuses on the result of a poor tee shot or a three-putt, they are focusing on something that they cannot control. When they focus on the present they are in problem-solving mode and allow themselves the ability to evaluate and understand what's important now. They also determine what areas of their game needs an on course adjustment in preparation for the next hole. During practice the focus is usually on the process: adjusting your grip, green reading, determining your yardage by club, etc. During a tournament, the key is to let go of the result and get back to focusing on the process.

2. Unrealistic Expectations

In tournaments, many golfers expect to always hit the ball clean whether from the tee, the fairway, or around the green. Some golfers show little tolerance when they mishit the ball into hazards or penalty zones. Conversely, a golfer usually expects to make mistakes in practice and use his mistakes as a learning tool. In fact, mistakes are a vital part of development. In essence, the golfer is allowing himself to fail and evaluate how once they correct their mistakes they are putting themselves in a better position to reach their goals. When discussing the sport of golf, one-time PGA Tour winner, Jason Gore, said, "You're dealing with failure a lot." Golfers should expect to make mistakes during competition. Rather than channeling their energy into that ball laying in the sand or the putt that just lipped out on the previous hole, they should focus on the process of the adjustments they need to make just as they would in practice. This is a vital part of playing golf and competing on a consistent level each and every time you step onto the course. Remember, mistakes are a part of the game—if they weren't, every fairway would be wide open and straight with no sand traps or huge water hazards to throw you off. It's how you deal with those mistakes and move forward that will set you apart from your competition.

3. Poor Time Management

In practice, golfers will often rush through drills allowing little time to incorporate routines or to even discuss with their coach the purpose of each drill. It is important to take ownership of your time during practice. Utilize it as a means of putting yourself in varying situations and lies that you may face during a tournament. Practice your routines before each

swing of the club. If you like to step away from the ball and take a deep breath then adjust your glove before addressing the ball, do that in practice. This built-in similarity to course-like situations will help golfers bridge the gap between practice and tournaments.

4. Nerves: Golfers are rarely nervous in practice

This is because they are not judging themselves nor is anyone else. During a round of golf or a tournament, golfers tend to find themselves bringing their attention to the judgement of the fans, the other golfers, etc. As a result, they begin to worry about the result of their on-course execution. They focus on uncontrollable factors in their game. It's also important to remember that if you are nervous, so are the opposing golfers! Golfers at each and every level get nervous. Think about one of the best golfers of today, Justin Rose. Justin once said, before winning the title at the 2012 WGC at Doral, "I think the most important thing to realize about playing under pressure is it doesn't mean you're going to play badly; the day I realized that, especially with putting, you know, even though you're shaking over a putt, doesn't mean you're going to hit a bad putt. So, it's nice to feel that heat. It's what we practice for, you want to be in these situations and it's important to remember that." Practice for any situation and you will be prepared when the time comes. Nerves are perfectly normal, just use them for good, don't let them beat you.

5. Trying to Impress Others

In practice, players focus on improving and performing the drills that their coaches are working with them on. During rounds in a tournament, all of a sudden there are others watching. Club championships, collegiate scholarships, and team selections such as the Ryder Cup are examples of some opportunities that are on the line during tournaments. Golfers often lose focus on their process and instead worry about impressing the people that are observing them. Conversely, they start thinking about what aspects of their game they need to showcase in order to impress. This may include a golfer over-swinging on the tee because they are focusing on attempting to bomb their drive. A golfer may also worry about criticism from a parent or coach for not performing well. In all cases, the golfer's focus is no longer focusing on the process. It is key for golfers to recognize when they lose their focus and refocus on the present moment.

Why Can't I Play Rounds Like I Practice?

In martial arts, they do not differentiate between practice and matches—everything is called practice. This is the same in yoga. The point is that we are always trying to improve and get better. So, while tournament rounds are different from practice, what would happen if you viewed it as a practice? A place to learn and get better!

List three things that you focus on in practice...

1. _____

2. _____

3. _____

When you focus on these things, what do you notice? _____

_____

_____

_____

_____

List three things that you focus on during your round... _____

1. _____

2. _____

3. _____

_____

When you focus on these things, what do you notice? _____

_____

_____

_____

_____

What is the main difference between practice and your rounds? _____

_____

_____

_____

_____

What things would make sense to let go of when you play your next round? _____

_____

_____

_____

_____

What things that you focus on in practice would be helpful if you focused on them during your round? _____

_____

_____

_____

_____

Workout 14
Mental Point

With an understanding of what you can and cannot control it is important to note that an athlete will inevitably lose focus. Rather than getting angry at one's self the key response is simple: awareness and acceptance.

Concentrate!
Focus on What You Can Control

What the Pros Are Saying

"…from a mental standpoint, I was as good as I've ever been. I never let myself get ahead of myself. I never thought about what would happen if I won, what comes with it. I wanted to execute every shot, I wanted to stay in the moment. I wanted to stay within myself."

—**Gary Woodland**, *U.S. Open champion*

"Sometimes you just get beat even when you play good. You've got no control over that."

—**Greg Norman**, *Two-time Major champion*

"A bad attitude is worse than a bad swing."

—**Payne Stewart**, *Three-time Major Champion*

Key Principles

1. The outcome is not something you can control.
2. Focusing on uncontrollables creates tightness.
3. Everyone loses focus. Recognize when this happens and refocus.

Concentrate!

We have all heard the phrase, "He/she got caught napping!" It happens when a golfer loses focus and slices the ball into the woods on an unobstructed shot. It has happened to every golfer in history. One moment you are concentrating and everything feels smooth, relaxed, and in control…Then boom! The next moment you seemingly find yourself walking off the green with a double bogey and your head hung low because your mind was in the past or looking into the future. It makes you feel as though you have been thrust into another reality. One where you feel tense and every step feels like a weight is on your back.

Or perhaps you have experienced this in a different way: You're a chip and a putt away from closing out the tournament. The only thought that is running through your head is that once you hit the chip, all you have left will be a tap-in par. You begin to press. Your heart rate goes up and you begin rushing your swing mechanics. Next thing you know, you bladed the chip over the green. Now you need to regroup in order to lessen the damage. You are left to wonder how your concentration strayed from "one swing at a time" to seemingly everywhere except the present!

Concentration is one of the most important and misunderstood mental skills. Tiger Woods has what he calls his "Cocoon of Concentration." When asked to describe it, he said, "I just get into my own little zone, my own little world, and there really is nothing that is outside of that. I get so dialed in to what I'm doing, that it feels like time slows down. I feel very comfortable in that moment… it's just crazy to just be in that position, but it feels like, whether it's the zone or whether you perceive it another way…it may be happening really quick, but also happening really slowly at the same time, it's kind of neat."

The dictionary defines concentration in a couple of ways: first, giving something your undivided attention; and second, narrowing focus. These are well written definitions but are a bit limited for an athlete. The competitive athlete needs to create an action plan, and more importantly, to apply it to their sport and their given situations.

My mentor, Dr. Alan Goldberg, a nationally known sports performance consultant, says, "Concentration is the ability to focus on what's important, and let go of everything else." This definition implies that an athlete may be concentrating, but if it's on the wrong thing, it won't be helpful. Taking Dr. Goldberg's definition, a step further, let's now define it as "The choice to focus on what you can control, and let go of what you can't control." Have you ever found yourself focusing on something you had no control over? Think about that situation. What did it do to your anxiety level? How did it affect your concentration in your downswing? Focusing on something we cannot control almost always will take us off course and quite literally off of the course. It creates a sense of helplessness and unease ultimately leading to a downward spiral. Conversely, focusing on something you can control, such as your energy level, your attitude, and how you react to a tournament situation will yield more confidence and control over your destiny.

There is a helpful strategy which golfers can use to help them concentrate on what they can control before each tournament. Try this exercise: on the left side of a sheet of paper list behaviors and strategies that you can control during a tournament and label it "controllables." Your list might include preparation, staying positive, adjustments, breathing, how you react to certain situations, or even bouncing back from adversity. On the right side of the paper, list what you are unable to control—such as weather, course conditions, or the outcome (you cannot directly control this or you would simply always win). Simply by labeling what you can and cannot control, you will have increased your awareness of where you want your focus to be. For example, a golfer cannot control the wind, but they can control how they

react to it and those adjustments needed to be made to ensure each shot is taken with thought and precision. Without this awareness, a golfer will continue to focus on the wrong thing.

With an understanding of what you can and cannot control it is important to note that an athlete will inevitably lose focus. Rather than getting angry at one's self the key response is simple: awareness and acceptance. This non-judgmental process will help the athlete reframe their focus.

Another element of proper concentration is to understand that a strong focus on something 100% of the time is not always necessary. In fact, it can be exhausting and can even lead to burnout. Knowing when to let go, release your focus and the accompanying pressure is a skill. This may be any time prior to, during, or after competition.

In summary, when viewing concentration through the lens of what you can control and what you cannot, it will become more manageable to play at the best of your ability. A golfer can always benefit from learning to refocus effectively rather than attempting to maintain being dialed in. In fact, letting go will perpetuate even stronger concentration by providing a more relaxed focus and will lead to more consistent performances each time they tee it up.

Concentrate!

Concentration: kan(t)•sen•'tra•shen: noun:

A. the act or process of concentrating; the state of being concentrated; especially: direction of attention of a single object.

B. to bring or direct towards a common object. To draw together and meet in a common center; to focus one's power, efforts or attention.

How would you define concentration in the context of sports?_____

_____

_____

Inside the Zone definition of concentration: *The ability to focus on what is important, and let go of everything else.*

Translation:

The ability to focus = The choice to focus

on what is important = on what you can control

and let go of everything else = and let go of what you can't control

New complete definition (write it in):_____

_____

_____

_____

_____

What percentage of the time during a round do you concentrate on what you can control? _____

And what percentage of the time during a round do you concentrate on what you cannot control? _____

Name a time during a round when you were concentrating on the right thing:

_____

What was the result? _____

Name a time during a round when you were concentrating on the wrong thing:

_____

What was the result? _____

_____

Understanding this new definition of concentration, and the above, how could this change things for you? _____

_____

_____

_____

_____

 **Lee Westwood** ✔
@WestwoodLee

Just gotta shrug it off and get on with it. The game was never meant to be fair. That's the mental challenge.

8:03 PM · Mar 7, 2021

Workout 15
Mental Point

Proper preparation will keep you relaxed before teeing off. It will enable you to stay calm and will allow you to unleash your natural talent when the round starts!

Rituals That Work
Plan and Prepare for the Next Round

What the Pros Are Saying

"A routine is not a routine if you have to think about it."

—**David Love Jr.**, *Former PGA Tour player & father/coach of David Love III*

"Tension and tempo changes the golf swing more than anything else, so noticing grip pressure, tension in arms and shoulders, etc. should be an integral part of your pre-round warm up and then maintaining it during your round."

—**David Mackenzie**, *Golf mental coach*

"At first, you probably let the dollars get into your head and you screw up and it costs you a lot of money. You get tired of that happening and start treating the last putt of the day the same as your first putt of the day."

—**Kevin Streelman**, *Two-time PGA Tour winner*

Key Principles

1. Rituals help an athlete feel prepared.
2. Rituals create a sense of familiarity.
3. Rituals allow the athlete to have control over a situation.

Rituals That Work

You cannot control the future—however, you can prepare for it. I love this saying because I consider it to be an important concept to remember before a big tournament. Any golfer or fan has heard about on-course routines (see Workout 17). But what can you do 24 to 36 hours before the big tournament? The answer is—a lot! It is important to understand that this is not the time to make technical swing changes. However, this is the time when mental preparation is key.

Think of it this way—if you were a pilot, you would have a checklist of all the things you needed to double-check before takeoff. If you were a carpenter, you would "measure twice and cut once." The same goes for sports! The main goal at this point is to be relaxed so that your natural talents, skills, and intuition can just flow during the competition. Hence why the focus should be on what you need to do to clear away all the potential distractions that can get in the way before your round.

Almost all golfers, both professional and amateur, have rituals to get themselves ready for the tournament ahead. Jason Day has a 15-step routine before taking his stance to hit each and every time. Rory McIlroy sticks to a strict diet and practice regimen leading up to a tournament. These types of routines or rituals lead these golfers to have a sense of calm before teeing off. The remainder of this workout will highlight key actions that should be part of your pre-tournament ritual.

1. Pre-Round Checklist and 'Altar'

During the evening before a tournament, it is important to lay out and load your golf bag with whatever you are going to need for the competition the next day. My wife, Debbie, a marathon runner, refers to this as "laying out her altar." It is her process to ensure she has everything that's necessary to compete and that she won't have to run around the day of the competition in a panic trying to find something at the last-minute. Proper preparation also ensures that the day of the round you are relaxed as it eliminates the need to complete another last-minute task. Items for the altar might include rain gear, extra golf gloves, socks, a sandwich and snacks, extra water, lip balm, etc.

2. Sleep and Hydration

Hopefully, you have been banking enough sleep and hydrating yourself leading up to the tournament. However, it is imperative to get to bed early the evening before a round. Most adults need eight hours of sleep for a great sleep; however, kids usually need ten hours. Plan this into your evening and work backwards so you can bank enough sleep. Also, I always recommend hydrating leading up to the tournament and keeping water by your bed. We all dehydrate when sleeping, thus the idea is to keep that to a minimum.

3. Pre-Round Strategy and Notes

On the night before or morning of a tournament go through your yardage book notes about the course and develop a strategy. Lock it in and then visualize yourself performing that strategy. You might also visualize specific situations that may arise on certain holes and imagine yourself adapting and adjusting to the situation. It is key to understand that adversity can rear its ugly head each time you step on the course to compete. It could be a tough lie in an old divot or rainy, windy weather or who knows what. Preparing for uncontrollable elements and visualizing how you will handle them under pressure will better prepare you to handle the situation when it occurs.

4. Stretch and Warm-Up

This step is often overlooked. Certain circumstances may prohibit you from being able to hit a few balls on the range or hit putts on the practice green, which then makes the stretching part that much more important. The idea is to get your body warm and your mind moving while remaining relaxed. One exercise that I love to use is to visualize some of your best shots from your own personal highlight reel—so to speak. If you're familiar with the course you're on that day, run through some of your highlights of your prior rounds! This will provoke thinking about your strategy and getting mentally engaged for competition. It will also incorporate muscle memory into the mix.

5. Tranquilo

So often this step is ignored yet it is so helpful toward achieving a relaxed balanced mindset. Just before your round is not the time to be concocting new strategies or devising new technical adjustments. Notice that many golfers prepare with their headphones on. Find what works to relax your mind.

Utilize these five rituals to prepare for success. Proper preparation will keep you relaxed before teeing off. It will enable you to stay calm and will allow you to unleash your natural talent when your round starts!

Rituals That Work

Pre-Round Checklist

A pilot, prior to take-off, will methodically go through a checklist to ensure the plane is properly equipped with the right supplies and will run smoothly. Similarly, a mentally ready player will go through their golf bag and clubs to ensure everything is in order with the proper supplies for an important round. Improper preparation will immediately put you a step behind.

The first few items you cannot put in your golf bag: rather they are intangible things that only you can control…

1. A good night's sleep on the nights leading up to your round, and especially the evening before (eight hours minimum)!

2. Drink water leading up to the tournament to hydrate your body.

3. A positive, problem-solving, and happy attitude.

Bag Check:

1. ___Extra golf balls/tees

2. ___Towels

3. ___Water

4. ___Banana/fruit snacks/PB & J

5. ___Rain gear and umbrella

6. ___New gloves

7. ___Sunglasses/sunscreen

8. ___Ball marker "that means something to you"

9. ___Sharpie to mark ball

10. ___Bagtags

11 ___Something that makes you smile ☺

Workout 16
Mental Point

What if you could improve your game by simply asking yourself— and thoughtfully answering—a few questions? Would that be worth it to you?

Stay Positive!
Seven Questions to Stay the Course

What the Pros Are Saying

"I used to really think about it a lot (winning tournaments), stay up at night, and think about why I haven't done better. I just quit thinking about it…Not in a sense that I don't care, but I can't do any more than how I work, and the time in the gym, and the tournaments I play—and I play a lot—I just can't do anymore. Grinding on it, I don't think it helps anybody."

—**Charles Howell III**, *Three-time PGA Tour winner*

"That day (2018 PGA Championship), I learned where the stage is the biggest, the noise the loudest, the pressure the most intense—that you could still control what you can control…I learned a whole hell of a lot. That round made me 10 more years a veteran. I wouldn't have been able to hold on at Pebble if I hadn't been in that situation with Tiger on Sunday in St. Louis."

—**Gary Woodland**, *U.S. Open Champion*

Key Principles

1. Beating yourself up is never helpful.
2. Nothing changes unless you make it change.
3. Be curious about what's happening.

Stay Positive!

How many of you take lesson after lesson hoping to learn the one technique that will give you the edge you're looking for? And how many of you read all the key golf publications looking to glean one or two valuable instructional tips? Most people probably answered "yes" to these questions. But what if you could stop beating yourself up and improve your game by staying the course and asking yourself—and thoughtfully answering — 7 questions? Would that be worth it to you?

The authors of 'Every Shot Must have a Purpose,' Pia Nilsson and Lynn Marriot, speak about self-awareness and knowing your game. Specifically, they share, "The key is to determine what works for you. It is important to learn to trust your instincts. People think that decision making is merely gathering information and then making a decision. It is much more than that. A key component of the information you gather is the self-awareness to understand what will work best for you. By playing the think game you can learn more about what works best for you, and the more you know about what works for you the more committed you will be to the shot you are going to hit."

I have provided seven questions below that will help you stay the course while highlighting areas for improvement in a purposeful, growth-oriented way.

There are always areas in which golfers excel and playing to their strengths are critical. For example, the 2007 Masters Champion, Zach Johnson strategically decided that on the four par 5's he would lay up on each second shot. He factored in his lack of length off the tee, cool temperatures and gusty winds . His self-awareness of his game allowed him to then capitalize on his strengths, the short game. He led the field with 11 birdies and zero bogeys on those par fives. Similarly, by identifying your strengths you can use them as the foundation on which to build a solid developmental plan. Starting with a positive outlook you are more likely to make changes and it becomes easier to identify what is missing from the ideal picture.

Ask yourself:

- What part of my game is working?
- What is behind my overall success?
- If I could imagine the ideal round—a situation for which I would strive—what would it look like?
- What is the difference between where my game is now and where I want it to be?
- What steps do I need to take to get my game where I want it to be?
- What do I need to do and/or do I need help?
- When can I start working on this?

Stay Positive!

What am I doing in my game that is working? _____

_____

What is behind my overall success? _____

_____

If I could imagine an ideal shot or situation—what would it look like? _____

_____

What is the difference between where my game is and where I want it to be?

_____

_____

What steps do I need to take to address these differences? _____

_____

_____

What do I need to do and/or who can help me? _____

_____

_____

When can I start taking action? _____

_____

_____

The Journey starts with a single swing...

Section 3
MID-ROUND WORKOUTS

Mid-Round Workouts

It's Not Personal

My performance and talents *are not mine*

But light that comes through me.

My body is a vessel that allows, blocks or hinders this light

My goal isn't to play well; it's to get out of the way

Understanding this, takes pressure off of me

As nothing is personal, it just is.

—**Rob Polishook**, *Author of* Golf Inside the Zone

Workout 17
Mental Point

The pre-shot routine helps us stay calm, centered, and maintain a consistent level of composure. Having your own pre-shot routine in place helps to manage pressure situations and better embrace challenges as a result.

The Pre-Shot Routine
Don't Leave Home Without It!

What the Pros Are Saying

"I never hit a shot, even in practice, without having a very sharp, in-focus picture of it in my head. It's like a color movie. First I "see" the ball where I want it to finish, nice and white and sitting up high on the bright green grass. Then the scene quickly changes and I "see" the ball going there: its path, trajectory, and shape, even its behavior on landing. Then there's a sort of fade-out, and the next scene shows me making the kind of swing that will turn the previous images into reality. Only at the end of this short, private, Hollywood spectacular do I select a club and step up to the ball."

—**Jack Nicklaus**, *Eighteen-time Major Champion*

"I´m getting close…it´s about focusing on my process…Each week I´m learning something…it´s not about returning to the old Lydia…it´s about being the best Lydia I can be today."

—**Lydia Ko**, *Two-time Major Winner*

Key Principles

1. A pre-shot routine keeps you organized in what otherwise can be chaos.
2. A pre-shot routine helps you stay focused on what you can control.
3. A pre-shot routine should be personal and meaningful.

The Pre-Shot Routine

In sports, and in life, athletes are required to perform under pressure. It is part of the game. Think back to a time you experienced a high-pressure situation. How did you manage it? Imagine that you are at the Masters on Sunday about to tee it up on the final hole. You are tied for the lead and know that if you can put yourself in position for a birdie on this final hole, a green jacket may be in your future. How would you handle it?

Whether it's a win at the Masters, club championship, or even a fun day on the course with friends, we always encounter challenges and pressure that go with it. More importantly, what is your pre-shot routine for staying calm and present in these situations? More often than not, high-pressure situations can make us feel tense, anxious, and sometimes hesitant.

Pre-shot routines are personal processes that each athlete uses to help them stay calm, centered, and prepared for the next shot. This routine is your opportunity to step back into your bubble where you can control things. It might seem like a small act, but the routine is extremely empowering for any golfer. The pre-shot routine will take a golfer's mind off of what they cannot control and focus in on what they can control.

On the course, your pre-shot routine remains a valuable tool. Utilizing your pre-shot routine during a round will help you let go of the previous shot or hole and get yourself properly prepared for the next one.

The pre-shot routine that I teach has four stages:

The first is the acknowledgment stage. This entails simply making yourself aware of what has already happened during the previous shot. This includes the good and the bad. Once you are aware of your current situation you can then facilitate change.

The second stage is your centering stage. Here you should bring attention to your breathing. The purpose is to bring your focus to the present moment and balance your nervous system.

The third is the strategy stage. Here you decide what your options are and the best way to approach your next shot.

The last stage is the physical routine. The purpose of this stage is to help you gain control with a familiar action and subsequently establish your rhythm.

The bottom line is that competition is full of pressure. A pre-shot routine helps us stay calm, centered, and composed. Having your own pre-shot routine in place helps golfers to manage these situations and better embrace challenges. The goal of a pre-shot routine is to refocus and move beyond the stress towards your goals. By creating a pre-shot routine and implementing it we bolster our physical and emotional preparedness.

The Pre-Shot Routine

Name a player whose pre-shot routine you like: _____

Describe what their pre-shot routine looks like: _____

_____

_____

How do you think it's helpful to them? _____

_____

_____

How could a pre-shot routine be helpful to you?_____

_____

_____

Create your own unique pre-shot routine _____

_____

_____

_____

_____

_____

_____

_____

Workout 18
Mental Point

**Here is the good news! We are all
born in the present, and have the
ability to stay in it and play in it.**

Tense, Nervous...Can't Relax?
Four Ways to Manage Pressure

What the Pros Are Saying

"I'm sure I'll come out and be nervous on the first tee, but that's what you want...If you are not nervous on the weekend you either missed the cut or you are playing for 71st place. So, it's good to get some mojo back and get some nerves going over the weekend."

—**Stephan Jaeger**, *Korn Ferry Tour pro*

"Your mind races...It's the greatest feeling. That nervousness."

—**Phil Mickelson**, *Five-time Major Champion*

"Being tense ruined more golf shots for more players than anything else I know. If and when you are all tightened up you just aren't giving yourself a chance to swing properly at the ball. Tenseness causes a lot of difficulties but the worst is that it forces you into hurrying and harrying your backswing."

—**Sam Snead**, *Seven-time Major Champion*

Key Principles

1. Everyone feels fear. It's what you do with it that counts.
2. Pressure isn't bad, it just is.
3. If it were easy, everybody would be doing it.

Tense, Nervous...Can't Relax?

How many times have you heard that the secret to playing your best is by being in the present? Have you ever experienced being inside the zone? Conversely, how many times have you experienced being *outside* of the zone where your thoughts were focused on the past, the future, or even others' expectations of you? For example, you might be preparing to hit your shot on a short par 3, but your mind is thinking back to the prior round when your ball landed in the water short of the green or maybe your mind keeps returning to a terrible putt you made on the hole before. Have you ever caught yourself playing in the future, where after shooting below par on the front nine your mind travels to the idea that this is going to be a great round? In fact, you think you are going to win the tournament with a ten under score! Sure enough, in all three cases, by being in the past or in the future, the results were adversely effected. Why is this? It is actually pretty easy to understand. If you're playing in the past or the future you have one eye on something you can't control and the other on the round. Certainly, this is no recipe for success! Once your attention is divided your play will suffer.

So, the bigger question becomes: What are some things you can do to help yourself focus on the present task at hand while you're competing? Once you become aware that your focus is in the wrong place then what are some pressure-release practices that you can use to calm yourself, get centered, and simultaneously bring yourself back to the present moment?

Here is the good news! We are all born in the present and have the ability to stay in it and play in it. To remain in the present takes discipline, awareness, and the desire to not attach to counter-productive thoughts such as missing a key putt that cost you a tournament. Interestingly, sometimes change is more frightening to a player than continuing to spiral out of control. How often have you witnessed a golfer with that "deer in the headlights" look, letting a round slip away stroke by stroke without any attempt to change tactics? Hence the saying, "it may feel good to swim with an anchor, but the weight of it is going to constantly drag you down."

It is helpful for a golfer to use pressure-release practices (PRP) in tight situations once things seem to be getting out of control. These PRPs are designed to take your mind off the fearful or anxious situation and refocus your attention on the present. In this refocused state, you can calmly focus on what needs to get done and swing by using your natural, instinctual game instead of over-thinking about technique, the past, or the future.

The following are four pressure-release practices. You will notice they are called *practices*, not strategies or techniques. This is because they are meant to be practiced both on and off the course. By practicing these they will become familiar to you and will enable you to access a sense of calmness in a quicker and deeper fashion. One of my clients explained to me that when she brought her focus to her breath at first it took a minute or so to calm herself. However, as she practiced the routine before bed each night, she reached a place where as soon as she asked herself, "Am I breathing?" it triggered a calming response.

1. Routine

Routines can be very effective for athletes. They are comfortable, consistent, and provide the player a sense of control and familiarity. There is little left to chance, allowing for a more singular focus. Serious golfers should create a routine that they can practice the evening before their round. This might include a familiar meal routine, preparing their clubs and gear, and some relaxation exercises to help them prepare for the tournament ahead instead of stressing about it. Another recommended routine is deciding what to do between shots. This pre-shot routine (see Chapter 17) may include some breath work (described in point 2, Breathing), designating an area on the course that serves as a positive space, or recalling an inspirational moment where you had success in a previous situation.

2. Breathing

I strongly advocate using your breath as a centering and calming practice. By bringing your attention to your breath and noticing its sound, feel, or rhythm, you will automatically bring yourself to the present moment. The simple act of doing this, of even asking yourself, "Am I breathing?" will take your mind off the pressure, help you release stress, and bring your attention to the present. There are many different breathing techniques from which to choose. Find one that you are most comfortable with. The key here is that your breath is always in the present. Attaching to your breath will help you detach from the stress, create a sense of calm, and put you in the best position to play the next shot.

3. Anchors

An anchor is something to which you can bring your attention, such as a memory, an inspiration, or a designated place on the course that is calming. The key to this practice is that the anchor brings about positive and safe feelings. It may be the feeling of hanging around the beach or being with a certain someone. The idea is that this anchor is connected to a feeling that facilitates a sense of calm in your body. For instance, the thought of the ocean is often very calming for people. Focusing on this often helps a golfer let go, release pressure, and center themselves. Your anchor should be personal to you, and just the thought or vision of it should lead to a sense of warmth, calm, and safety.

4. Be curious, not furious

This one may sound funny, but just the act of being curious puts you in the present without any preconceived judgments. Being curious creates a sense of awareness of what is happening around you, without thoughts of the past or future getting in the way. Try this: instead of being angry or even ecstatic at your result be curious about what happened. When you are curious you usually become more in-tune and open to what is going on around you. You will also find yourself becoming less judgmental of the situation which then allows you to respond in a calmer fashion rather than merely reacting quickly.

Try these pressure release strategies and see which ones work best for you. The key to all the practices is that they allow you to move away from the stressful situation and offer a sense of calm in return. Once you have attained the calming effect, you can then bring your attention back to your round and you will be able to strategize in a clear and directed manner. Remember, these are called practices for a reason: that means you can practice them every day for a few minutes. Over time they will become as comfortable and familiar as a glove when you use them on the course.

Today you are You,
that is truer than true.
There is no one alive
who is Youer than You.

—Dr. Seuss

Tense, Nervous...Can't Relax?

In this chapter, I have addressed ideas that can help you slow down, change your focus, and relax during tense situations (routines, breathing, anchors).

Let's briefly explore what can happen in a tense situation. Oftentimes a player will describe their heart speeding up, not feeling certain parts of their body, trembling or shaking and generally feeling inclined to speed things up. On the other hand, players in the zone describe it as relaxed, time slowing down, and swinging the club effortlessly.

Our energy goes up and then naturally comes down like a wave in the ocean, that is unless a fear, anxiety, or situation threatens us and we spike up (freeze). What is important to understand is that the thought is not the problem; it's when we react to the thought. For example, I missed that shot, then taking it a step further to mean I'm going to lose.

When fears and anxiety enter your mind, practice not reacting to the fear, but rather just being curious to it. Not adding anything to the emotion, just be aware of it. Usually it will go away.

Anchoring Exercise:

Step 1: Think of a time or experience in your round where you faced adversity but overcame it. Describe it. _____

_____

_____

_____

Step 2: When you think of it, notice how you feel. Describe it. _____

_____

_____

_____

Step 3: Imagine a situation in the future which may make you feel tight or nervous. Describe it. _____

_____

_____

_____

Step 4: Now, imagine the time from Step 1 where you turned things around, just noticing that centered, competent feeling . . . _____

_____

_____

_____

Step 5: What do you notice? _____

_____

_____

_____

Now, go back to the situation that may make you tight or nervous. You may notice that by changing the focus to a feeling of accomplishment (overcoming adversity), the nervousness of the future event may subside and not be as intense as before.

Workout 19
Mental Point

Effectively managing pressure is a counterintuitive process. Rather than ignoring the pressure it is necessary to accept it. Acceptance neutralizes pressure and helps to take the edge off.

Tension, Tears, and Twitches
The Secret to Managing Stress

What the Pros Are Saying

"I loved how he (Payne Stewart) played the game certainly as a competitor but then how he lived his life off the golf course—he's the model. It's about how you utilize the gifts you're given."

—**Zach Johnson**, *Two-time Major Champion*

"It means so much to get a win, and it gets you into so many different tournaments and solidifies your job for two more years. That's enough pressure for anybody."

—**Michael Thompson**, *Two-time PGA Tour winner*

"Don't harbor things internally. Don't push the elephant under the rug. Anxiety and happiness both come from within. And so, you have to ask, which one do you prefer?"

—**Greg Norman**, *Two-time Major Champion*

Key Principles

1. Everyone gets nervous; it's how you manage it.
2. Just be You!
3. When you are tense, slow down and notice your breath.

Tension, Tears, and Twitches

How many of you get nervous waiting to hit your first tee shot in front of a crowd? How many of you can feel the pressure standing over a putt to close out a tournament? Nerves play a key part in golf and in any sport. Nerves can make an athlete physiologically tight. Here is what can happen to a golfer when nerves set in: they will get a surge of adrenaline in their central nervous system, their heartbeat pounds like a drum, beads of sweat start forming on their skin, their breath gets short and shallow, their muscles contract, and their blood pressure increases.

Effectively managing pressure is a counter-intuitive process. Rather than ignoring the pressure it is necessary to accept it. This acceptance neutralizes it and can take the edge off. This is much like the well-known "elephant in the room" scenario that we all encounter at one time or another. Rejecting, ignoring, or denying that the elephant exists simply leads to greater discomfort. Only upon the acknowledgment that stress exists in the mind are we able to reduce the tension.

A common misconception is that the top players don't feel nerves, tension, anxiety, or fear. Take top pro golfer, Bubba Watson, for example. Watson has been dealing with a lot of anxiety both on and off the course. He was once asked about it and he responded, "I had a lot of noise in my head…I've sought help in many different ways, many different forms, trying to overcome it. It really all comes down to me being nuts. I'm trying to make light of it because using humor helps. But it's all in my head. It's all anxiety."

There are mental skills that the great players utilize to thrive despite such emotions. These players are able to effectively accept these emotions as part of their individual process and consequently don't attach to them. This is so they can play in a place of focused awareness. How many times have you heard a golfer say, "If only I didn't choke on that last putt, with the lead, I would have won!" The reality is that you cannot separate the mental game from the tactical, technical, and strategic game. They are all interrelated, critical components that surface in high-pressure situations and the top pros know it.

Media, fans, coaches, caddies, and even golfers often misunderstand nerves and how to manage them. It is common to hear a statement such as, "champions don't like to admit to nerves." In many cases this may be accurate, but it seems that some elite players are not afraid to express how they experience their emotions. Dustin Johnson, after his U.S. Open win at Oakmont in 2016, was asked about how he can seem so nonchalant on the course and if he felt nervous at all when competing and said, "It means something to me, the day you're not nervous on the first tee is kind of when it doesn't mean anything to you."

In order to keep his anxiety at bay on the golf course, Jordan Spieth finds solace in chewing mint gum. While he was holding a two-stroke lead at The Open in 2017, he said, "I was one under through two holes and I thought I better keep it in and it's still in now. It's probably time for a new piece…Payne Stewart used to do it and it served him well, but I think mint has some sort of effect on my nerves." Whether or not mint gum it has any scientific effect, it has surely helped Spieth remain calm under pressure! On the other hand, if it kept his nervous system relaxed, loose and flowing, certainly I can see where it would help.

Professionals and amateurs are often discouraged from being honest about their emotions and are consequently compelled to fight an internal battle in order to deny what they are feeling. Mind you, it is one thing to openly publicize your nervousness to your opponent, but the real trouble comes when a golfer does not privately allow themselves to acknowledge what they are experiencing. When a golfer fights emotions, their focus stays on the emotional state (inducing concern or panic over what they are suppressing), rather than accepting it for what it is and making the choice to move on. Resisting an emotion's existence only makes it stronger. Think elephant in the room!

Jackie Burke Jr., currently the oldest living major champion at 97 years old, knew nerves existed in his game but also knew the importance of keeping them under control to see success. "You never see a surgeon nervously juggling knives before an operation. You're going to trust that? No. You have to take tension out of your swing. The key to my golf was the four T's: tension, tempo, timing, and trust." It's ok to have nerves, but use that knowledge to your advantage, and have trust in yourself to non-judgmentally experience the tension.

In conclusion, a machine-like mentality to ignore nerves is misdirected. In fact, it pushes athletes farther from peak performance because they are scared to be themselves and to fully acknowledge their own mental and emotional experience. Great athletes instinctively understand a key mental edge secret—it is okay to have nerves. In fact, accepting the experience of tension is the first step towards releasing it.

Tension, Tears, and Twitches

The Secret to Managing Stress

When was a time you were feeling stressed or nervous on the course? _____
_____

Does this happen often? _____

What did you do? _____
_____
_____

What are some things you could do to help release the tension and refocus? Hint: Refer to previous chapters for more pressure-release practices; i.e. breathing.

1. _____

2. _____

3. _____

4. _____

5. _____

How could this help you? _____
_____
_____

Workout 20
Mental Point

The best players in the world have doubts, fears, and nerves as we all do. It happens to everyone. The question becomes how will you respond, play through it, and avoid the negative downward spiral?

I SUCK!
How to Tame Negative Self-Talk

"Well, I am still in shock that I did that…I just can't believe that I did that. I am such an idiot." (2006 U.S. Open)

—**Phil Mickelson**, *Five-time Major Champion*

"It's just one of those things, I believe in myself and—especially with how hard I've worked…"

—**Patrick Reed**, *Masters Champion*

"Whatever chances I had I threw them away on the back nine; I just went brain dead. My body just didn't react to my thoughts, I couldn't think straight and didn't make any good decisions."

—**Sergio Garcia**, *Masters Champion*

Key Principles

1. Look at what's happening, not what happened.
2. Negative self-talk comes from a part of you that is scared.
3. The secret to managing self-talk is to notice it but not get caught up in it.

I SUCK!

All competitive players recognize negative self-thoughts. It starts with that devilish little voice in our head that raises doubts, fears, and questions about our ability to perform. The little voice usually comes during the most pressure-packed times during a round. It's that voice that says, "I suck! I'm pathetic!" after a missed approach shot, or "How could you do that again?" after another errant shot. It's that cynical little voice that whispers, "If you double bogey again you're going to lose this tournament," or, "I wonder what my friends and parents are thinking now," after you miss a short putt. Negative self-thoughts precede negative self-talk. Without proper awareness, negative thoughts can bring even the most competitive golfer down.

When a golfer chooses to listen to their negative self-thoughts and begins negative self-talk, that is when the downward spiral usually begins. It often plays out like this: A golfer mishits a ball which they expected to hit without fail and in their head the little voice of doubt enters and begins chiming in. Simultaneously, their body starts to get tight. Instead of moving on to the next shot, stepping off the ball, or any other form of refocusing, the verbal self-talk begins and the golfer continues to harp on the past, verbally berating themselves. All of this leads to tight muscles, loss of feel, and further errors.

What is important to understand is that we have a choice regarding whether to react or respond to our negative self-thoughts. When we react to this devilish little voice with defensiveness, and deny its existence, the voice gets louder and louder. There is a saying—"What you resist persists." By trying to deny this voice or feeling, it only wants to be heard even more. It is also important to understand that just because you conjured up this negative self-thought does not mean that the thought is true. For example, have you ever been at the brink of losing a tournament, had a negative self-thought, such as "It's over; I'm going to lose," only to bounce back? This is because you accepted this thought not as true or false or as a validation of anything but just non-judgmentally. As a result, the thought just faded away and you were able to play the hole like any other.

So…what can a golfer do when they get bombarded with negative self-thoughts, especially in the thick of a tight round when under pressure? If the golfer is aware of the self-thoughts and the patterns they can make the choice to step away and change their focus. The following six practices can be used when negative self-thoughts start creeping into your head and negative self-talk begins to spew out of your mouth.

1. Be aware and watch it dissolve away

The problem is not the negative thoughts—those are normal. Don't resist it or fight with it. Instead, simply understand that it is a by-product of being in a high-pressure situation. With awareness of these thoughts, take a step back, bring your attention to your breath, and visualize the thoughts being released with your exhalation.

2. Welcome and normalize

Say "hello" to the negative thoughts—by acknowledging them, you normalize them. You can actually say to thoughts, "Hey, thanks for sharing your concerns but I'm in the middle of a round. Go back to the cart." You might also pretend that your favorite comedian is mimicking this reply, which may bring humor to the situation.

3. Put a time lid on it

Here again, the concept of acceptance comes through. If you find yourself muttering "I stink" after a shot or tournament, rephrase that by saying, "I stunk on that shot," or, "That was one bad round." Even after a tournament concludes, many times a kid will come off the course sullen and saying, "I suck." While ideally the young golfer would not feel this way to begin with. A realistic and far healthier approach would be, "I may have sucked today, but tomorrow is another day."

4. Reframe the situation

Imagine that you are on the 18th hole and need to jar a ten-foot putt for the win. You are ready to address the ball. The thought comes up: "Uh oh, I'm so nervous." Ask yourself: "What is another way of looking at this?" How about considering the challenge and opportunity to hit a great putt to win? Instead of dwelling on the obstacles associated with our nerves we can shift attention to the process that entails what we must do to overcome them.

5. Change your focus

You hear those negative thoughts; it feels like you are about to be swallowed up by a wave. This is the time to change your focus. Bring your attention to your feet or your breath and just be curious. This five-second distraction may be enough to help you calm down and regain your concentration.

6. Towel off

The towel is a great reason and excuse to take a moment to regroup. It provides a break from the action and a time to just let go. Today's golfers always have a towel on hand in their bag and it is not just to mop up sweat!

In summary, we all have negative thoughts yet when you sense them escalating to self-talk you need to regain control of the situation. The best golfers in the world have doubts, fears, and nerves just as we all do. It happens to everyone. The question becomes how will we respond, play through it and avoid the negative spiral downward? When in doubt, go back to the six practices when you have those I suck negative thoughts.

I SUCK!

The Art of Talking to Yourself!

We all talk to ourselves...you know that little inner judgmental critic that says "you shoulda done this," or "you coulda done that." Sometimes the critic even calls you names! "I'm an idiot" or "I can't believe you did that!"

Can you recall a round when you were highly frustrated?

Describe the situation: _____

_____

_____

With that round in mind, list all the negative things you thought or said aloud. (Be honest!)

1. _____

2. _____

3. _____

4. _____

5. _____

Looking at this list, what does it make you aware of? _____

_____

How did saying these things affect your confidence and performance? _____

_____

_____

Would you say these things to your best friend? _____

Why not? _____

_____

_____

What could you do to bounce back from the mistakes? _____

1. _____

2. _____

3. _____

How would this be helpful? _____

_____

_____

Inhale/Exhale...
Breathe!

Workout 21
Mental Point

How many of you can recall a time you were on the course and lost your focus due to an unexpected bounce—or even a misread putt on a fast green? The real challenge is to regain your focus in order to get back to a place of calm.

You Cannot Be Serious!
Seven Tools to Help You Regain Your Focus

What the Pros Are Saying

"If I can get my mind in a good place, that's going to help me more than anything else…It doesn't mean I will, but at least I'll know I did everything possible."

—**Christina Kim**, *Three-time LPGA Tour winner*

"I'm 24 years old, so a lot of the things that happen to me are things that I am experiencing for the first time…The more you put yourself in situations the more comfortable you get and the better you are able to handle them."

—**Kyle Stanley**, *Two-time PGA Tour winner*

"I just want to play golf, man…It's simple…Just stay in the moment and keep plugging along"

—**Brooks Koepka**, *Four-time Major Champion*

Key Principles

1. Expect the unexpected.
2. You will inevitably lose your concentration, what's important is to bring it back to what you can control.
3. The most important moment is the NEXT moment.

You Cannot Be Serious!

Some of the greatest golfers have lost their focus while on tour. Sergio Garcia has been known to get upset and toss his clubs. Sergio even was seen throwing his shoe into the crowd at the 1999 World Match Play at Wentworth. Tiger Woods has also been known to curse in frustration. Despite losing their focus for a moment, these golfers are also known to be some of the best to regain their focus. Losing your focus is not the end or even a problem unless it leads to a continual spiral downwards. However, what's important is being aware that you lost your focus and refocus on what you can control.

Now it is one thing to see a professional lose their focus. However, the question is how many of you can recall a time you were on the course and lost your focus due to a topped three-wood, a bad bounce—or, even because of a putt you missed that you thought would be as easy as throwing a seashell into the ocean? The real challenge is regaining your focus in order to bring yourself back to a place of calm where you are able to play the next hole free of distractions.

It is important to understand that you must be aware of having lost your focus in the first place! It sounds simple, even obvious. With awareness you can choose to respond to the adverse situation by slowing down and making the choice to refocus. Be aware that it takes courage to change your focus from where you were and reach a place of calm. In challenging situations try using the following tools to regain your focus and stay on track:

1. Routine

The power of routines are that they are predictable actions that a golfer can rely on to feel more comfortable during an unpredictable situation. For this reason, routines will help to bring you back to a place of calm. Jason Day infamously has a 15-step pre-swing routine to get him ready. Jim Furyk addresses his putt then lines up his putt before stepping away from the ball to get one last look from behind. These actions keep the golfers comfortable and in control. Routines focus our attention on the "here and now."

2. Self-coaching

With self-coaching, golfers ask themselves questions that result in physiological responses. For example, there are a number of questions you can ask yourself, such as, "If I were relaxed, how would I feel?" or, "If I were having fun, what would it feel like?" Inevitably, your body's natural physiological response will be to release tension, become curious and return to the present moment.

3. Reframing thoughts

Much like self-coaching, reframing your thoughts requires that you assess the immediate situation and employ alternative techniques to help you stay calm. For example, you may find yourself saying, "Oh no, here we go again! I always screw up. I'm going to double-bogey this hole." Rather than fighting these thoughts, try reframing them. For instance, say something like: "I hear you, but now is the time to concentrate," or, "Yeah, this is a pressure-packed moment so hang on for the ride." Remember, it is okay to be nervous—it is even natural. All pros admit to having nerves. However, the champions are the ones who accept the nerves and then continue playing rather than suppressing their nerves and freezing up.

4. Anchors

Before a round create and choose an anchor that makes you feel calm. It might be a song, the feeling of relaxing at the beach, or the emotions you feel when you're with a loved one (pets included). When things get rough during the round, focus on recalling the sounds, sights, and feelings you associate with that anchor. By allowing yourself this mental break you return to the course with a fresh outlook on the game.

5. Cue cards

Before a round prepare a cue card with a few pertinent words, phrases, or quotes that may help you relax. Write statements on the card such as: "Focus on fairways," "I don't have to be perfect," or simply "Breathe." Then, attach the cue card to your towel or golf bag. Refer to the ideas on this card before each hole for inspiration and a feeling of calm.

6. Breathing

Bring your attention to your breath—the body and the breath are always in the present moment. By simply noticing your breath's natural rhythm, either the sound or the feel of it, you will bring yourself into the present and calm will usually follow. Sometimes noticing your breath can be too tricky or passive an activity for some golfers and they become impatient. If this happens to you, remember to breathe in relaxation and breathe out stress. Say or think the words as you do this. Another breathing exercise is to inhale to the count of three and exhale to the count of four. You might even discover your own breathing rhythm when you hit the ball.

7. Eye-of-the-hurricane focusing

To use eye-of-the-hurricane focusing simply bring your attention to an object and focus on it. This narrowing of your focus will help you eliminate outside distractions. You may want to focus on the sound of the ball off your club or even the sweat dripping from your brow. Once you are focused on your object of choice you can then begin to expand your focus and take in everything around you. You will find this narrow-to-wide focusing to be very calming.

You Cannot Be Serious!

Tools to Help You Regain Your Focus

The idea behind concentration is not necessarily to focus 100% of the time, but to know when you have lost your focus and regain it. Try the exercises below for five minutes each.

NO DISTRACTION EXERCISE:

Step #1: With your eyes closed, notice your breath as you inhale and exhale.

Step #2: As you inhale, visualize the number 1; as you exhale, silently say the number 1. Repeat this process.

Step #3: If you get distracted or lose focus of the number 1, gently move on to the number 2 and visualize the number 2.

What number did you reach? _____

What did you do when you lost your concentration? _____

_____

DISTRACTION EXERCISE:

Now, let's incorporate distractions. Turn on the TV, or have a friend try to distract you. Either way, close your eyes and follow the no-distraction protocol. Expect to lose your focus many more times.

What number did you reach? _____

_____

How was this different? _____

_____

_____

_____

Is it bad that you're losing your focus?_____

_____

The answer is no: What is important is understanding that you will lose your focus. What's key is bringing your focus back to what's important and what you can control at that time. It's impossible to focus 100% of the time. The top pros know how to relax and then focus at key times.

When you lose your focus, what are two things you can do to regain it?

1. _____

2. _____

Workout 22
Mental Point

Losing focus is a natural occurrence; the key is being aware that you lost your focus and bringing it back to the present.

Save Par? Relax...But How?
Five Steps to Closing Out a Tournament

What the Pros Are Saying

"I played really solid golf. I think I only had three bogeys all week. Just really stuck to my game...allowed my putter to speak volumes." (2020 3M Open)

—**Michael Thompson**, *Two-time winner PGA Tour*

"If you worry about making bogeys, it makes the game that much more difficult. You put pressure on yourself without even noticing it. It makes a difference to take it easy when things aren't going right."

—**Sergio Garcia**, *Masters Champion and Ryder Cup veteran*

Key Principles

1. If closing was easy everybody would be doing it.
2. An opponent is most dangerous when they have nothing to lose.
3. Closing out any round is difficult—expect that!

Save Par? Relax...But How?

How many times have you found yourself in a tournament in which you were just a few strokes from winning? Maybe you have a two stroke lead on 16 and you began to think, "Oh my gosh, this is great. I'm going to be the champion!" or, "Only one last hole and the trophy's mine!" In another situation, you might be even closer to the "finish line." Maybe this time you are leading by 1 stroke with one last crucial hole when you begin to think, "Just one more hole!"

All weekend warriors, tournament and professional players have had these thoughts. The question becomes: How many of them have succumbed to such thoughts and went on to lose the tournament or round? The answer is, many! Look no further than Greg Norman in the 1996 Masters when he led by 6 after 54 holes. He was positioned to be Australia's first Masters Champion. However, Norman's game collapsed as he shot 78 and lost to Nick Faldo's 67 in an 11 stroke swing. While it is true that many professionals and top-ranked golfers may lose their focus during critical times during a round, the truly mentally tough competitors become aware when this happens and are able to regain their focus.

Paradoxically, losing focus is not horrible. In fact, it is a natural occurrence; the key is being aware that you lost your focus and then changing it to bring yourself back to the present. The problem is that when it is happening you may swear that you are concentrating and you probably are—just on the wrong thing! Focusing on the events of the future immediately removes you from the present moment and takes you to a place where you have no control. Furthermore, as your thoughts drift into the future, you lose touch with what is really important and what brought you to this point: playing without thinking, relying on your feel and natural instincts, and trusting your game—the game that got you to this moment in the first place.

So, what can a golfer do? No doubt this is a difficult situation but by employing the following five mental-toughness strategies—especially when you find your game spiraling out of control—you can give yourself the opportunity to get back in rhythm and turn things around.

1. Become aware

The first step to combating loss of focus is to become aware that you have indeed lost it. When we talk about "concentration" in the sports arena we are referring to the choice to focus on what you can control and let go of what you can't control. All golfers lose their focus at times; it is inevitable. The truly mentally tough players, however, understand this. They don't beat themselves up when it happens, and they immediately bring their focus back to what they can control.

2. Refocus on the present

This is imperative but how can you do it? First off, know that it takes a lot of courage and discipline to mentally refocus. However, what is the alternative? A free-fall! To refocus, bring your attention to your breath. Your breath is always completely present: just listen to it and its rhythm, sound, and feel as it enters and leaves your body. Or visualize yourself breathing relaxation in and breathing stress out, slowly letting go of the stressful air as you visualize it dissipating as on a cold morning. Another present-moment awareness exercise is to breathe in through your nose to the count of three (if possible) and out through your mouth to the count of four. Or make up your own pattern. These relaxing breathing patterns will help you to stay calm, relaxed, and mentally present during the most difficult transitional moments of a round. Other present-moment exercises to try includes visualizing the feel of a shot, your rhythm, target zones, and the contours of the greens. These can all act as "anchors" to make you feel calm.

3. Change focus

Inevitably golfers tend to lose focus when they think about the future such as what might happen on the next hole. The key here is to recognize this loss of focus and bring yourself back to your next shot.

4. Let go of winning and of expectations

Remember, you cannot control whether you win or lose, or whether or not you knock down a winning putt. Likewise, you cannot control the expectations others have of you. Paradoxically, the harder you try to close out a round, the more physically tight you will become. Just play each stroke the best you can; if you do this, you will put yourself in the best position to win. If you do not win, you can walk away feeling positive about your effort.

5. Trust the process

Bring your attention to what you must do to execute properly on each hole, which might include staying relaxed, managing the course strategy, or knowing your comfort level with each club. Ask yourself what it would feel like to hit a great drive. Your body knows; now is the time to trust it. Then ask yourself what it would feel like to play this hole relaxed and instinctively you will feel a release from stress.

Using the strategies above will help you succeed on the next hole, round, or tournament. This is because they help you to begin the hole in a calm and relaxed place. Remember, save par...relax!...now you know how!

Save Par? Relax...But How?

Try Softer, Not Harder

One of the biggest mental traps that athletes fall into is **"trying too hard." Fueled by frustration** or making the contest too important, trying too hard is usually a game of diminishing returns: The harder you try, the worse you'll do!

This is because **you put pressure on yourself**, rush yourself, and your **muscles tighten up**.

Peak performance always comes from being in a **state of relaxed awareness**, a place of letting go, where the actions happen without much conscious effort or thought.

When you become aware of **yourself trying too hard**, pressing, or rushing…**Shift your focus** of concentration away from the outcome or its importance to the present task at hand.

Remember you want to **relax and try "softer," not harder**.

What does the passage above make you aware of? _____

_____

How does this apply to your game? _____

_____

In order to try softer, not harder, what are three things you could do?

1. _____

2. _____

3. _____

Workout 23
Mental Point

As a golfer you are unable to directly control bad lies or bounces because you are unable to control golf course conditions. However, you can control how you address your ball and decide which club best suits your next shot.

The Towel is Your Friend
How to Stay Calm Before Each Shot

What the Pros Are Saying

"I've made big strides in the last two weeks to get from kind of a panic place to a very calm, collected, and confident place. It's difficult to do in two weeks. Sometimes it takes years. I feel like I've been able to speed that process up a lot over the past couple of weeks."

—**Jordan Spieth**, *Three-time Major champion on his 2018 Masters performance*

"Every moment on the course, like every moment in life, is to some degree unique and unrepeatable…Tryin' too hard is the surest way tae (to) ruin yer (your) game."

—**Shivas Irons**, Golf in the Kingdom *by Michael Murphy*

Key Principles

1. Let go, relax, the next shot will still be there.
2. Use the towel to refresh and refocus.
3. Pros use the towel all the time…Do you?

The Towel is Your Friend

How many times have you seen the pros toweling off during a round? Often professional golfers will towel off between each shot. Some may have the towel strapped to their golf bag ready to go whenever its needed. Many reach for the towel as their last routine before getting into their stance. Others will have their caddie on stand-by to hand it over as soon as the shot is finished. Regardless of their idiosyncratic method pros use their towel(s) for much more than it appears.

When you are playing in a tournament, how often do you reach for your towel? In tight situations, do you take the time and walk over to your towel to give yourself a break from the action? We all see in professional tournaments that the pros have the luxury of the towel being handed to them by their caddie.

The towel can be your best friend on the course. In addition to the fact that it mops off the perspiration on your face and arms, your towel is much more than you may have realized! It is a built-in stress reliever, a separation from the pressure of the round. No, it's not like going to your favorite ice cream shop or the beach, but it can provide you the necessary time you need to relax, bring your heart rate down, slow your breathing, and most importantly, decompress and get yourself centered for the next shot. As a routine, retrieving your towel breeds a familiarity that keeps you comfortable on the course and helps you stay in the present. It also can help you control the pace and rhythm of the round.

You are unable to directly control your score because you are unable to control the golf course conditions. However, you can control if you walk up to the tee with a clear mind or not.

So next time you play that long grueling par 5 take the time to retrieve your towel. Wipe off the sweat, clear your mind and take a break. Incorporate the towel into your pre-shot routine. Whether for your brow or your club, the towel can help keep you focused on the objective ahead by giving you a few extra moments to breathe.

The Towel is Your Friend

The Towel is Your Friend

Most pro golfers towel off between shots. Is it because they sweat more than amateurs? Hardly! They know what most junior players do not…

The towel is your friend. It can help you to:

- Slow things down
- Catch your breath
- Relax and get centered
- Compose yourself
- Let go of the previous shot
- Wipe sweat off your head and hands!

How about also attaching an index card to the corner of your towel? On the card can be a quote or phrase that motivates you or a few things which you want to remember. They should be non-technical things which will provide you insight, help you relax, and motivate you. They should also be customized to the specific round, course, and circumstance.

For my index card I usually write things like:

What are your key points?

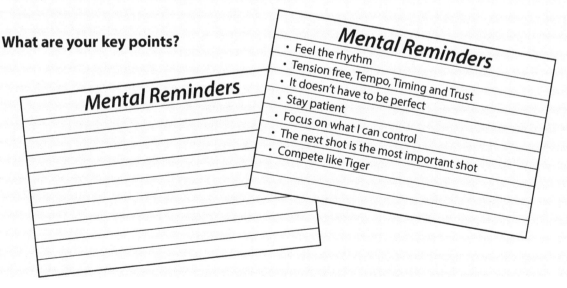

Mental Reminders

Mental Reminders
- Feel the rhythm
- Tension free, Tempo, Timing and Trust
- It doesn't have to be perfect
- Stay patient
- Focus on what I can control
- The next shot is the most important shot
- Compete like Tiger

Workout 24
Mental Point

The key to competing is adapting and adjusting to what is currently happening.

Competing Against the Field
One Part Skill, Three Parts Will

What the Pros Are Saying

"In the past…I put too much pressure on myself. I went out there and I tried so hard to get the ball in the hole. I tried so hard to hit perfect shots going into this week I was just like, 'Hey, it's golf, go play.'"

—**Patrick Reed**, *Masters Champion*

"I think that I'm kind of just doing what I usually do and go out there, keep it simple, and have fun, and remember it's just a game and whatever happens, happens. But I'm pretty confident in myself, and know that I'm going to be out here for a long time. So, I don't need to be putting all that pressure on one shot or one missed cut."

—**Matthew Wolff**, *One-time PGA Tour winner*

"…I think having those past chances that I wasn't able to convert…got me ready for this moment. Going into the back nine my caddie and I just really wanted to stick to our game plan, stick to the process of just being really engaged on each shot. And we were able to do that." (2021 Valspar Championship

—**Sam Burns**, *First-time PGA Tour winner*

Key Principles

1. Play proud.
2. Your opponent is the course, not the enemy.
3. Play within yourself, not without!

Competing Against the Field

It's 101 degrees and the sun is beating down with no cloud cover in sight. The air is thick and moist and the course is as hard and dry as the Sahara Desert! I feel the heat throughout my body as I look for shade cover. I see a sliver of shade behind an oak tree that sits just before my approach shot. I've been out here for nearly 4 hours and I'm the co-leader entering the final holes. I remember what my coach said: *"Closing out any tournament is one part skill and three parts will."* At this point, I know it's all about how I compete. I'm thinking, "What do I have to do on this final hole to put myself into position to win?"

In between shots I reflect back and remember the hours of training I put in at the range, on the putting greens, lifting weights, and conditioning myself for these moments. I also think of all the mental training I have practiced. Ugh, exhaustion is setting in. I wonder if I even have enough energy left in me. It is decision time. Either I push through and compete or give in and fold. Another thought crosses my mind…why I am doing this in the first place? Yet I have made it my motto to compete to the fullest each and every shot of each and every round. *I remind myself to bring my attention to my breath—it's so simple, but always seems to calm me and bring me into the present.*

This round has been a battle—the momentum swings have been like waves in the ocean, one after another, relentlessly crashing over each other. I still cannot believe how my playing partner played out of his mind on the front nine. Okay, that is well beyond my control now. It is time to start my pre-shot routine on the 18th tee! Every swing is important. I remember my coach saying, *"The key to ideal competing is adapting and adjusting to what is currently happening."*

The sudden wind shift requires an essential change in strategy to pull out this hole and the tournament. I have honors on the tee. This time I'm choosing my 3-wood over the driver to land short in order to avoid the fairway bunker. Not my typical strategy on this hole, but reaching the green from that bunker is too difficult to risk. I'm confident that I can place it short and I will still have a perfect approach towards the green. I remember my coach saying, *"The ability to be aware of what is going on in a round and be willing to change strategy when necessary is what separates the top 1% of competitors from the other 99%."*

The sun and humidity has me a bit light-headed, but there is nothing I can do except try to hydrate and manage my energy for just a bit longer. I've battled for four hours and understand that despite my best preparation I cannot control the way this round has affected my body. My mental training coach says, *"There are many things that you can't control, such as: You can't control how your playing partner plays or acts. You cannot control the sudden wind that just picked up that will affect your ball flight. You cannot directly control the result of this round—you can only control yourself, the shot selection you choose, and how you handle your emotions."*

I'm feeling like a fragile warrior pushing through all the potential distractions. Is this how Arnold Palmer felt when he came back from a seven-stroke deficit to shoot a 65 in the final round to win the 1960 U.S. Open? Both Ben Hogan and then amateur Jack Nicklaus were in contention.

I remind myself to stay focused on what I can control in my tournament. My job is to get myself in a position in which I can stay within myself on the next shot in a calm, centered place. I use my breath to help me stay in the present and relax.

My 3-wood lands in the fairway just short of the dog-leg and fairway bunker. I need to hit a knock down approach into the stiff wind. My opponent gambled with his driver off the tee and landed in the fairway bunker with a plugged lie. I can see that he's getting uncomfortable and restless. My ego tells me to go for the flag, but I know I have to push this aside. Just hit the center of the green. I cannot worry what other people think about my strategy as that is just another uncontrollable. I must do what I think is best to win and put aside any other concerns.

Good news…my opponent is rattled. He's called for an official to get a ruling on his plugged lie. I try not to respond to his antics. I cannot allow him to rattle me. My inner coach tells me…*Nothing is gained from being a poor sport. I try to find a balance of how to be a good sport as well as how to be a good competitor. The concepts are different, yet integrated. In order to compete at your best, you have to respect the game and your opponent. This mindset keeps me in a focused and centered place.*

For my approach shot, I chose a 7 iron knowing I'm about 170 from the pin into a one club wind. I hit a clean knockdown shot landing safely on the green setting myself up for a 24-foot birdie putt. My opponent, on the other hand, had to clear the lip of the bunker so he's short of the green. He'll have to get up and down from 75 yards and his short game is capable enough to pull that off. However, the strong wind left his approach well short of the green. He just about made par with his pitch shot, but putts out for a bogey. All I need to do is two putt and the tournament is mine. Easier said than done. However, I make a smooth and calculated stroke and I leave a tap-in putt for par and the win. It's over! We shake hands after my caddie gives me a big hug.

This win was not easy; it ultimately wasn't about skill, but about competing in the moment. I had to adapt and adjust to the round's momentum, focus on what I could control, and let go of what I could not. I had to battle without expectations, be willing to put my ego aside, and through it all I had to stay alert. These are the skills necessary to compete at your highest level.

Competing Against the Field

Pre-Round Intangibles Scale

This exercise will help you rate, become aware, and better understand key intangible factors prior to a key round. Rate yourself and against the field on each of these measurements (scale: 0 = not at all; 10 = very much). If you're unable to rate the field, complete the exercise only rating yourself.

Opponent: _____

Tournament: _____

Date: _____

Confidence	Myself	Field
Momentum coming into the tournament		
Experience factor		
Physical readiness		
Mental readiness		
Hunger factor		
Concentration		
Ability to focus on controllables		
Ability to manage uncomfortable situations		
Ability to make opponent uncomfortable		
Ability to stay emotionally balanced, and refocus		
Awareness		
Ability to compete		
Ability to stay the course (resilience, tenacity)		

Confidence	Myself	Field
Ability to bounce back from adversity/obstacles/setbacks (perseverance)		
Ability to adapt/adjust, switch plans (flexibility)		
Ability to make high-percentage choices		
Ability to play within self, take what the course is giving you (patience)		

What does analyzing the Intangibles Scale make you aware of? _____

_____

_____

_____

What are you aware of in relation to the field? _____

_____

_____

_____

From the above, what are three things that would help you as you prepare for your round?

1. _____

2. _____

3. _____

Workout 25
Mental Point

Success is achieved when a player can proactively ride out the wave and stay above water. The goal is to stay afloat—nothing fancy, just keep grinding. Just as the calm existed before the wave, the calm will resume after the wave has passed.

Riding the Waves
Using Momentum to Win in Competition

What the Pros Are Saying

"It can be hard when it's something that's the norm, when you've kind of been fighting through things for awhile…It's a process coming back. Any time I get a chance on the weekend and especially anywhere near contention to kind of see where things are, then I'm able to make adjustments and improve from there."

—**Jordan Spieth**, *Three-time Major Champion*

"I much prefer when it's tough…Guys aren't necessarily too happy when it's tough and level par can move you up spots, which is what I like. You've got to grind, and I'd rather stick in rather than just being sort of relaxed and going at every pin. I don't like that type of golf."

—**Matthew Fitzpatrick**, *Six-time European Tour winner*

Key Principles

1. The struggle is part of the journey. Expect adversity.
2. Golf is like a roller coaster: Many highs, many lows…just hang on.
3. It's not how you start, but how you finish.

Riding the Waves

A surfer paddles out to the open ocean. The water is calm, the surfer is in complete control. Atop his surfboard the surfer can enjoy the tranquility of his sport. However, he has not come out to the open water to enjoy tranquility. The surfer has ventured out in search of the big wave—the wave that will get his adrenaline pumping; the wave that will satisfy his craving for the thrill of competition; the wave that will push him to the absolute limit. He has come not for relaxation but to embrace a challenge. (Think of the aptly named Bonzai Pipeline!) The surfer looks forward to the biggest wave that may come his way. When the "big one" comes along it will undoubtedly test his physical abilities, challenge his mental game, and for a moment leave the surfer wondering if he can come out of the wave unscathed. But if he does, if he stays on the surfboard and is able to ride the wave out, he will be ready for whatever comes up next. If he cannot stay on the surfboard, he will spiral out of control, be thrashed under the water, and have no ability to take advantage of calm seas or handle a new wave.

There are parallels between this anecdote and a golfer competing in a tournament. Just like the surfer, a golfer may begin a round in complete control. They make the shots they are supposed to make and par the holes they are supposed to par. But then, just as a wave is bound to occur in the open ocean, a change and momentum shift is bound to occur in a golf tournament. This is the natural evolution of nature and sports. Consistency plays a small role in both. The wave is impossible to stop—the momentum cannot be controlled. The best strategy is to continue to battle and try to ride it out.

A surfer may see a wave approaching far in the distance, just as a golfer senses a change in momentum before it shows on the leaderboard. The wave may show itself either as a let down in one's own game, i.e. poor mechanics on a shot, bad read of the green or as a boost in your opponent's game, such as stringing consecutive birdies while clicking on all their shots, etc. Factors beyond the player's control, such as poor weather, tight fairways and slippery greens can also lead to a momentum swing. These situations are inevitable in a tournament. But given the players' level of awareness of the specifics in a round, and their ability to sense the upcoming waves of momentum, golfers have the opportunity to mentally hunker down and prepare themselves for the impending change. There are times when the waves may be so sudden that all the golfer can do is hang on, grind it out, and hope to stay afloat.

Metaphorically, the wave is a change of momentum often out of the golfer's control. Your opponent may sink a long, winning putt on 18 while your putts have lipped out. The only hope to get through the wave is to ride it out. The wave should not be viewed as a setback or even an obstacle, but rather as an opportunity. An opportunity to test one's ability to remain focused, level-headed, and in control. An opportunity to adapt and adjust one's game to what works best in changing situations and to push oneself both mentally and physically towards eventual success.

But success can only be achieved if a golfer can proactively ride out the wave and stay above water. The goal is simply to stay afloat—nothing fancy, just keep grinding. Countless times Tiger Woods has demonstrated his ability to do this by matching his opponents and staying ahead hole after hole. Just as the calm existed before the wave, the calm will resume after the wave has passed. The question becomes: is the golfer still on the surfboard, or have they let that wave throw them off? If they are on the surfboard they are in a position to battle once the wave and momentum passes. However, if the golfer feels sorry for themselves, cannot stop thinking about past shots, and is despondent about the negative turn of events, they will be completely unaware that the wave has passed. They will continue to spiral out of control. The golfer will not be able to take advantage of the newly found calm after the storm.

A golfer must recognize that momentum shifts are unavoidable in competition. It is just part of the rhythm of a tournament. Just as waves in the ocean ebb and flow, the momentum of a round constantly changes as well. This is a natural phenomenon and the reason why we find sports so entertaining. Waves, momentum shifts, and adversity in a tournament should be seen as a challenge, something to be embraced. Perhaps LPGA Golfer, Inbee Park, said it best, "This is what I love to do. And if pressure is something that comes with playing golf, that's something a professional golfer has to handle."

In the end, riding the big wave is the ultimate thrill. A surfer may struggle with the wave but stay on the surfboard and ride the big wave to shore. Or they may completely fall off the surfboard and capsize. When the surfer stays calm under pressure they can persevere no matter how big and how many waves come their way. Once the surfer knows he can handle the waves, he can embrace even bigger waves, and hope for even bigger challenges. Only through challenging oneself and confronting increasingly bigger obstacles can you improve. No one's saying the wave will be easy to ride out. The object is to battle it and stay afloat. Only by embracing the challenge of a big wave, and testing one's limits, will true potential be uncovered. Remember, nothing great is ever achieved without overcoming adversity.

Riding the Waves

Hello–Goodbye Exercise

Pretend you are playing the front nine. Each hole will be an opportunity for you to embrace something (say hello), and an opportunity to let go of something (say goodbye). For example, say hello to the nervousness of people watching and say goodbye to the fear of being judged.

Now, as you imagine playing the round, continue to fill in the blanks.

FIRST ROUND

Example: Hello: _Nervousness of people watching_   Goodbye: _Fear of being judged_

Hole 1: Hello: _____   Goodbye: _____

Hole 2: Hello: _____   Goodbye: _____

Hole 3: Hello: _____   Goodbye: _____

Hole 4: Hello: _____   Goodbye: _____

Hole 5: Hello: _____   Goodbye: _____

Hole 6: Hello: _____   Goodbye: _____

Hole 7: Hello: _____   Goodbye: _____

Hole 8 : Hello: _____   Goodbye: _____

Hole 9: Hello: _____   Goodbye: _____

Score: Hello: _____   Goodbye: _____

Workout 26
Mental Point

Tournaments are not the time to analyze technique—it is the opportunity to simply play by getting "out of your mind" and allowing the body to do what it has been trained to do.

Get Outta Your Mind
It's the Only Way to Compete!

What the Pros Are Saying

"During my career, when I first started playing the game, sports psychologists weren't part of your team. But if I had the ability to trust someone to give me advice, or help me with my attitude, damn right I would have been a better player."

—**Greg Norman**, *Two-time Major Champion*

"Your final goal is to convert you're athletic swing to pure instinct rather than conscious thought."

—**David Leadbetter**, *Golf swing instructor*

"Quit competing…and you dry up like a peach seed."

—**Sam Snead**, *Seven-time Major Champion*

Key Principles

1. Remember your training; trust your instincts.
2. Overthinking leads to paralysis.
3. Listen carefully—your body knows what to do.

Get Outta Your Mind

We have all heard people say "She played out of her mind!" referring to someone who played exceptionally well and beyond expectations. As an athlete have you ever performed out of your mind? Perhaps by hitting every fairway, or landing your approach shots within tap-in distance, or you don't miss with your putter? Maybe there is more to this "out of your mind" concept than meets the eye. The idea is ultimately a metaphor for playing within yourself, where everything is effortless, where little thought occurs, and optimal performance just happens. I will describe how getting "out of your mind" is the best way to reach optimal personal peak performance in competition.

When a golfer plays "in their mind" they are not playing from instinct. They are usually over-analyzing and their thoughts are cluttered and disorganized and they interfere with their ability to play well. Further, their thoughts are in the past and future, tied to expectations, ego, excitement, and fears. Essentially their thoughts are weighing them down—athletes describe it as playing with an imaginary weight around their waist while trying to run, jump, hit, and concentrate while their mind is over-thinking every move.

We all know what happens when this kind of mentality creeps in the dreaded downward spiral where a golfer loses control! Physically and mentally it looks like an initial loss of focus, fear about what might be or what is occurring, tightened muscles, heavy breathing, and loss of feeling. Then the poor play follows usually ending in disappointment and defeat. The only way to optimize performance is to play in the moment (present) and to respond to situations with calm awareness as opposed to reacting out of ego, fear, and anxiety. I call this the "eye of the hurricane," calm on the inside yet aware and active on the outside.

The key to staying in the moment is within all of us—the secret lies in our bodies. Our body is always in the present moment. When an athlete becomes aware of their body, such as the stability they feel with their feet properly planted before they swing a golf club, they simplify things and enter a place of noticing what's happening. I call it observe more and narrate less. This moves them away from distracting thoughts. In fact, all of the "what-if," "shoulda-woulda-coulda" thoughts are no longer in the way because the focus is on observation rather than judgment. Essentially, by getting "out of your mind," you get "out of your way" and simply allow the technique you have practiced and your performance to flow in the present. If an adjustment is necessary it can then be made without judgment.

How can a golfer shift their focus from "outta their mind" (thoughts, past, future, comparisons and judgments) and into their body (present, feel)? The shift starts with awareness. When the golfer becomes aware of being submerged in over-thinking, fear or that recognizable downward spiral, the solution is to simplify things. Step back and shift one's attention to something in the present. For example, a golfer may focus on their breathing or a place in the body they feel calm and centered (a chakra perhaps). This refocus of "out of your mind" and into your body serves as a reconnection to the present— a place of calm and observation. From this place the golfer can play by observing and noticing instead of judging their technique or performance.

At the start of a round a golfer has the skills to compete at their personal highest level. The competition is not the time to analyze technique—it is the opportunity to simply play, by getting "out of your mind" and allowing the body to do what it has been trained to do. It is easy to let your mind creep toward the result, get caught up in expectations, question whether others are judging your performance, or dwell on the missed opportunity of a birdie. Yet the aforementioned tools can help the player to keep their attention out of the mind and in the present, and to be able to respond to the moment.

Golfers love those times when they feel immersed in the competition, competing effortlessly, and ultimately playing inside the zone. So during your next tournament shift your focus "outta your mind" away from fears or judgments and "inside the zone" to your breath and body and begin the path to unlocking your potential.

How to Feel a Real Golf Swing," by Bob Toski and Davis Love, Jr., with Robert Carney

Free arm-swing
Your goal: an arm swing as free and rhythmic as a child on a swing.

Get Outta Your Mind

The Frog and the Centipede

A frog was sitting on a patch of grass by his pond one sunny morning when a large centipede passed by.

The frog watched this creature with fascination, then said, "Excuse me, can I ask you a question?"

"Why, yes, of course," replied the centipede, pausing in his stride.

"I am amazed at the way you can proceed so harmoniously with your one hundred legs," said the frog. "Can you explain to me how you manage to keep them in order?"

The centipede reflected for a moment. "You know, I have never really thought about it," he said. "Let me see if I can demonstrate it for you."

And he started to walk, thinking about which leg should follow another. Immediately, he fell down and had great difficulty getting up again.

"You are dangerous!" he said to the frog angrily. "Never again ask such questions!"

After reading this poem, what does it make you aware of? _____

_____

How does this relate to your golf game? _____

_____

List three ways this insight can help your game:

1. _____

2. _____

3. _____

Golf Gods—
May they be
with you…

Section 4
POST-ROUND WORKOUTS

Post-Round Workouts

A Driving Passion

The thought that the game—and being a part of the game—could mean so much to someone is understandable.

It's what the game does.

It's how it works.

It's a part of its strange charm.

The feeling may not be true for everyone, but for many the game becomes a piece of ourselves. It's not who we are but it's a part of us and we like it that way.

It's why we make practice swings in empty elevators. Why we keep weather apps on our phones. Why we bet a steak dinner with a friend that he can't go a full year without buying at least one new piece of equipment.

It's why we imagine green sites in fields along the roads we drive and why people name their dogs – or children – Hogan.

It's why it's news when Augusta National announces it intends to allow a limited number of patrons to attend the Masters in April.

It's why when I say Rickie, you probably think Fowler. When I say Phil, you think Mickelson. When I say Bryson, you think cheeseburger.

It's a game in which the better you get, the harder it gets.

Regardless, when golf gets you, it tends to keep you.

Not everyone who plays gets it. They're playing the notes but not hearing the music.

Golf is a community, a curious one to outsiders but a treasured one to many of us.

—Excerpts from a larger piece featured in the *Global Golf Post* by Ron Green Jr. article titled: *A Driving Passion: golf lovers accept, embrace games gravitational pull.* 1/18/21

Workout 27
Mental Point

How do you cope with the disappointment? How do you bounce back from a painful defeat? First off, let's acknowledge: it's not easy and it hurts!

Double Bogey!
Five Steps to Dealing with a Tough Round

What the Pros Are Saying

"It's hard to take any positives from it right now…I'll sit down and reflect over the next few days and see what I could have potentially done better, whether it be a mindset, or, I don't know, I just didn't have it today." (2018 Masters)

—**Rory McIlroy**, *Four-time Major Champion*

"Do I think about it? (1979 Masters) Not as much as I used too. I don't dwell on it. I've never felt like, 'Why me?' You look at things that go on around the world, and other people's circumstances. What did I do? I missed a putt to win the Masters. If that's the worst thing that happened to me, even in just golf, so be it."

—**Ed Sneed**, *Four-time PGA Tour winner*

Key Principles

1. The only time you lose is when you give up.
2. Setback are an opportunity for a fresh start.
3. Failure is feedback and part of the process.

Double Bogey!

Imagine you're playing in front of a huge crowd of spectators grinding out the final round on a challenging course under the hot sun. You've outplayed your nearest opponent on the front nine. Then, starting off the back nine you carelessly double-bogey a short par 3 allowing your opponent to tie things up on the leaderboard. You're now coming down to the final hole even with each other. You've reached the green in regulation on 18 while your opponent came up short of the green. You get to witness your opponents beautiful chip shot from just off the green roll in center cup for birdie. Your birdie putt slides past the hole. You hear an echo in your head… "I've lost." It's another disappointing loss, coming down to an unlikely shot by your opponent. But this one stings even more as you had played the front nine to near perfection. Despite a few errant shots to start the back you kept it close the whole way. Slowly you walk up to the center of the green and shake your opponent's hand. Your hand feels limp and your body feels like the energy has been sucked out by a vacuum cleaner. You simply can't believe what has happened.

So, what's a golfer to do? How can you get over this disappointment? Your parents and friends tell you "it is nothing, just move on." "You will do better next time," they say. Don't you just hate that phrase?!

However, still covered in sweat and feeling partially paralyzed, you hear them, but can barely say anything. You feel as if you have lockjaw, unable to mutter a word. In your mind, you are still replaying the holes that you feel you should have won.

So, let me repeat…what's a golfer to do? How do you cope with the disappointment? How do you bounce back from a painful defeat? First off, let us acknowledge: It's not easy and it hurts! However, at some point, when the pain starts lessening, anywhere from a few hours to a day or so, it becomes imperative to view the tournament through another lens. That is, how do you begin to pick the pieces up? And what must you do next time to get better? How will you take advantage of certain situations and continually put yourself in a position to get over the hump?

The following are five steps to help you both experience and move past a disappointing performance. Equally so, this list is great for parents, coaches, caddies, and friends as they try to support the golfer during the process of disappointment, release, and rebounding.

1. A right to be disappointed

You have earned the right to be disappointed. Let's face It: after putting it all on the line and competing with all your heart, it is practically impossible to put on a smiling face and just forget things after a close loss. Give yourself some time. It's okay to be disappointed. In fact, it's even expected. Why wouldn't you be? You care, you practiced, you're a warrior, and you fought like one! Disappointment is a natural emotion—it even hurts, and that's okay too. It's not something that needs to be fixed. It is time that usually heals it. Allowing yourself to experience the disappointment you also allow yourself the opportunity to release and resolve the painful feelings. One of the things that makes victory so sweet and motivates us is knowing the feeling and experience of disappointment.

2. One step closer

Believe it or not, you are actually one step closer to your goals! Don't forget, slumps fit in here too. It may look like you're going nowhere, or even backwards, but keep on plugging away and learning. Harris English's return to the winners circle at the 2021 Sentry Tournament reinforces this concept. English went seven years without a win until his recent victory in Hawaii! He lost his Tour card in 2019 and then went back to the Korn Ferry Tour before rediscovering that if he just played his game and stopped being someone else he could still prevail. English once said, "I was thinking about what I can do to swing like them (DJ, Koepka, Rory) instead of thinking what I can do to make my swing be as good as it could possibly be. And I realized my swing can be just as good as any player's swing in the world."

3. Failure provides feedback

Failures, setbacks, and obstacles always throw us for a loop, but it's the true champion who can readjust and glean valuable feedback. Feedback should be viewed without judgment and as a learning opportunity in which you can make changes and adapt—adjusting to the situation next time. Think about it: Was there ever a great champion, individual, or team that didn't learn from failures, setbacks and obstacles? All great champions know why they are competing and use this "Big Why" to get themselves back on track. How long did fans judge Tiger Woods when he stopped winning Majors? They said he was all washed up. Eventually Tiger scaled the mountain top again on April 14, 2019 to win his fifth green jacket at the Masters. He used failure as feedback en route to his comeback.

4. Reframe it!

Simply stated, after you have decompressed, ask yourself the basic questions. What's another way to look at this loss or situation? How can I find something positive from it? What's the lesson here? Even though you lost, what can you learn? And don't forget: Give yourself some credit for showing up and putting yourself on the line. How many others are competing with such a heart as yours?

5. Focus on the process, not the outcome

This is probably one of the most important points and the major one that all other points can probably be folded into. While you lost this performance, it is another step toward your ultimate goal. The tournament gave you valuable experience and exposed you to the situational pressure of closing out a victory. This is highly valuable and can't be duplicated in practice. Remember, all great champions have to pay their dues.

The European Tour ✓ @Europ... · 17h ∘∘∘
What are the odds of a lie like this?!

Well, it happened today.

#ADGolfChamps #RolexSeries

💬 66   ↻ 63   ♡ 414   ↥

The European Tour ✓ @Europ... · 17h ∘∘∘
Tournament Director Miguel Vidaor explains what happened ⋯

Double Bogey!

First off...let's acknowledge that it hurts to lose, especially when you have put yourself on the line and tried your best in that specific situation and time. Second, let's acknowledge that it's hard to bounce back from a painful loss but you can do it!

What was a time you experienced a difficult final round? Describe it: _____

_____

_____

_____

What are three things you learned from the loss?

1. _____

2. _____

3. _____

How can you use these lessons in future tournaments? _____

_____

_____

_____

If you did, what would happen? _____

_____

_____

_____

Workout 28
Mental Point

You don't have to like failure,
in fact you can even hate it!
However, you must recognize it is
necessary for success. You deserve
to be disappointed and even angry
after a setback; however, this does
not have to be a permanent state.

Mistakes, Setbacks and Failure
The Only Way to Regroup

What the Pros Are Saying

"My father taught me the easiest thing to do was quit. He'd say, 'it doesn't take any talent to do that.'"

—**Ken Venturi**, *One-time Major Champion, 14-time PGA Tour winner*

"The best thing that ever happened to me was not winning the U.S. Open in 1960. Because if I had won that Open, I would have been too smug or too self-confident and felt like however I had prepared, my game was ready. But I was growing into the game then."

—**Jack Nicklaus**, *Eighteen-time Major Champion*

"It feels amazing (after winning a major tournament ranked #304), There's a lot of hard work behind it, and a lot of struggles that I went through the last 6 years. I'm just glad I was able to overcome everything and just keep my head in it…I knew I was capable. I just had a lot of obstacles thrown in my way, and I'm glad I stuck with it. I almost quit playing last year, so thank God I didn't."

—**Sophia Popov**, *Women's British Open Champion*

Key Principles

1. Failure is feedback.
2. It's not how hard you can hit, but how hard you can get hit and bounce back.
3. It's not whether you make mistakes, but how you rebound.

Mistakes, Setbacks and Failure

No one likes to make mistakes in practice nor encounter setbacks and obstacles and certainly no one likes to fail and lose in a tournament. It can be hurtful, disappointing, frustrating, and sometimes feels like you are back to square one! But there is a secret—a secret that only the top players know. Many top junior golfers fail to grasp what professional golfers, such as Tiger Woods, Dustin Johnson, and Rory McIlroy, have experienced and used to their advantage as they have developed into the best the game has to offer. This knowledge is that mistakes, setbacks, obstacles, and failure are inevitable. Furthermore, it is how a golfer learns and adapts from these difficult experiences that determines whether their potential is fulfilled. They don't allow disappointments to sidetrack them when striving towards their ultimate goal of continuous improvement and long-term success.

I would like to share an example of a golfer who was thought to be counted out. Ken Venturi, Golf Hall of Famer (2013) established himself as a top notch contender when he had three top five finishes at the Masters in 1956, 1958, and 1960. However, in 1961 Ken sustained minor injuries in a car accident that affected his ability to play golf that eventually led to his career tailspinning. During his 1963 season, Ken had won less than $4,000, had been dropped by all of his sponsors, and was mired in a terrible slump. Ken thought of quitting. Instead, he came back and won the sectional to qualify for the 1964 U.S. Open, a major that was expected to be won by several others. The 1964 U.S. Open was played in sweltering 100-degree Maryland heat. Venturi opened with 72-70 and was 6 back heading into the 36-hole, final day. Doctors urged Ken to stop playing after the first 18 due to dehydration and the risks of heat exhaustion. Needless to say Ken opted to play and posted a 66-70 score to win by 4 shots.

Success is like climbing a mountain—there is no such thing as a straight path. The player has to continually adjust and navigate switchbacks, pause at certain points, and even go backwards in order to find a path which can take them higher. Learning from failure and not letting himself quit led to Venturi coming back and finally getting over the hump.

This brings to mind a phrase I learned from my mentor Dr. Alan Goldberg: "Failure is feedback." This phrase refers to the idea that failure provides a valuable window for the athlete in which they can use the feedback from a negative experience to make necessary adjustments and changes in their game. These changes will get them back on the proper path towards their goals. However, without awareness of a golfer's own weaknesses the player will continue to do the same things, make the same mistakes time after time, and spiral downward.

You don't have to like failure; in fact, you can even hate it! However, you must recognize it is necessary for success. You deserve to be disappointed and even angry after a setback. However, this does not have to be a permanent state. Rather, by utilizing a heightened awareness of what happened you can begin to work through the things that may have gone wrong. You may have played poorly today, but that does not mean you will play poorly every day. Your future results are not set in stone. If you lost, that does not mean you are a loser, but you simply lost today; tomorrow is another day with another course to challenge. Additionally,

it is vital to understand that your main opponent is yourself and that the competition is there to help you gauge your progress and improve. Lastly, understanding that you are a work in progress and not a fixed entity opens the door for improvement, change, and different results.

The key point here is that winning is a process that is littered with setbacks, mistakes, obstacles, and failures. If approached with the right mindset an athlete will recognize these setbacks as temporary. They can learn from them and ultimately move forward towards their goal. The next time you lose, ask yourself: What can I learn from this? How can I use this experience to make an adjustment in strategy or technique to reach my ultimate goal? Remember, behind every crisis lies a far more valuable opportunity.

Have no fear of perfection— you'll never reach it. SALVADOR DALI

Mistakes, Setbacks and Failure

> "No one has ever achieved something great without encountering adversity. Mistakes are the portals to discovery."
>
> —**James Joyce**, *Irish writer and poet*

A mistake, setback, or loss is never the problem. The problem lies when we don't step back to learn from our mistakes. Mistakes provide feedback. The only mistake is not learning from it.

Next time you make a mistake, try not to judge it or yourself. Be aware of what happened and let it go. Trust yourself to make an adjustment the next time you're in the same situation.

List three mistakes you made in the last round you played:

1. _____

2. _____

3. _____

Choose one and describe how you judged yourself at the time. _____

_____

_____

_____

_____

What do you notice when you talk to yourself this way? _____

_____

_____

_____

What could you say to yourself after a mistake that would be helpful? _____

_____

_____

_____

Create a mistake routine. What short routine could you do to help yourself let go of mistakes? Describe it. _____

_____

_____

_____

Workout 29
Mental Point

It's important to remember you must focus on the present, compete, and let go of uncontrollable expectations. Just play!

OMG! I Cant Believe I Lost
Seven Mistakes the Favorite Makes

What the Pros Are Saying

"I just can't beat myself up, although it's going to be pretty hard not to, at least the rest of this afternoon. But there's a whole lot of nothing I can do about it right now. I just need to execute better when I get in that situation in the future." (2020 Workday Charity Open)

—**Justin Thomas**, *One-time Major Champion*

"I don't want to be mechanical. I want to be stepping up fast, hitting it and I want to be playing all kinds of shots and be the artist. But if you can feel early into the backswing that something's not correct, if your brain recognizes something is not correct, you just can't do that until you fix it."

—**Jordan Spieth**, *Three-time Major Champion*

Key Principles

1. Winning isn't just about technique, it's about how you compete.
2. Perfection is rarely required to win.
3. Let go of expectations, they cannot be controlled.

OMG! I Cant Believe I Lost

"I'm the better golfer, how did I lose?" Does this phrase sound familiar? Imagine the final round of an annual amateur tournament. The weather was hot, muggy, and the sun was beaming down like a laser. The time was 3 p.m. and the spectators, coaches, and local media surrounded each hole. The final pairing featured the heavily-favored local amateur, Sander Myles, and his opponent, Paul Robinson. They had never met before but many people suspected that Myles was the stronger player based on his reputation and ranking. Some people even suggested that Robinson played less risky and laid-up often on par 5s while he referred to himself as a competitor.

The round did not go as most expected. Myles, who had looked so self-assured on the range and putting greens, seemed surprised by the steady Robinson. At some point during the round Myles got a bit deflated. He appeared flustered with every swing of the club. He berated himself a few times and soon was shaking hands on the 18th green with his head down. The leaderboard showed Paul Robinson won handily by 4 strokes over Sander Myles. The kid Sander now looked shell-shocked. He had no idea how he could lose to a fellow with a swing like that. But one thing he did know was that Robinson never gave up, remained poised even when the lie was not great

and maintained a steady level of play until the last hole.

All tournament players have probably experienced this situation at least once in their competitive career. Yet how many of these players really seek to understand what happened and try to put a plan together so that history does not repeat itself in the next tournament? Likely too few.

This workout is intended to highlight the biggest mistakes a favorite can make against a supposed underdog.

1. Overconfidence

How many golfers have you seen begin a round feeling like they are entitled to win based on rankings, technique, or past results? The downfall with such a mindset is that focusing on off-course factors will take a golfer out of the present moment and distract them from performing their best during the round.

2. Focus on winning

We all want to win! However, it is important to remember that winning is not 100% in our control; we must also consider that we have an opponent who also wants to win. Whenever a golfer begins to think ahead to the result, he or she should change their focus away from the outcome and back to the process of the present moment—on something they can control. They could ask themselves, "What do I need to do to play this hole well?" It might start with focusing on their breath and getting themselves in a centered and relaxed place. (See Workout 11, "How to Play in the Moment: It's as Easy as Breathing.")

3. Listen to the hype

Your friends, teammates, coaches, and maybe even the media are going to be singing your praises. While these accolades are nice to hear, they will not get you a spot on the leaderboard. All your efforts should be on what you can do to prepare for the round. This mindset isn't glamorous, but if you listen to the true champions, this is how they approach each tournament. They focus only on what they can control, and let the rest go.

4. Rely on talent alone

Talent is great—it makes the sport easier to learn for some than for others. However, everyone eventually faces an opponent where talent alone is not enough to earn the victory. In fact, sometimes talent is a curse for a golfer who views his or her ability as "enough" to get results. Talent, work ethic, on-course intelligence, grit, and the will to compete are all crucial factors in player development.

5. Lack competitive intensity

If you ask anyone what percentage of a round is about competing and what percentage is about playing your best, the answer is that competing is more important. It is extremely rare that someone is able to play their best all the time. However, a golfer can always control how they compete.

6. Lose composure

Sure, if you are the favorite, everybody is expecting you to win. Therefore, when things get close, the underdog is inspired—while for you, the frustration kicks in. Before you know it, the negative self-talk starts, the club flies, and suddenly you have lost control on the course. The favorite must always be prepared to give their best effort, remain focused, and work every shot no matter the level of golfer they are competing against.

7. Awareness

Oftentimes the favorite is not even aware of what is happening on the course with regard to tactics and strategy. This is particularly the case because they have a preconceived notion of how the round should play out. Once again, their focus is on the past or future and they are playing to an ideal instead of playing in the present. It is important to play the round without expectations, except that you will compete fully and attempt to play your best. This open mindset will allow the golfer to see what is unfolding before them and to make the necessary adjustments.

OMG! I Cant Believe I Lost

When an athlete focuses on what they cannot control, stress goes up, breathing increases, muscles tighten, confidence falls, performance lowers, and slumps continue…this is because you have no direct control over these things. They change from moment to moment.

When an athlete focuses on what they can control, they will be more positive, relaxed, and open to opportunities. This is because the process is within their control.

Peak performance demands that an athlete focus on what they can control.

List controllables and uncontrollables for your next tournament.

Controllables	Uncontrollables
Preparation	*Weather (sun/wind/rain)*

What does completing the table make you aware of? _____

_____

_____

_____

How can you use it to help you? _____

_____

_____

_____

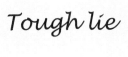

Tough lie

Workout 30
Mental Point

Whether a golfer wins or loses, they should always ask themselves some key questions about their performance. The goal is to raise awareness of what happened.

Sweet Victory!
Seven Questions to Ask After a Win (or Loss)

What the Pros Are Saying

"I always say, to some people, it's very easy to win with grace, it's a lot harder to lose with it."

—**Jean Van de Velde**, *Two-time European Tour winner*

"Winning never really crossed my mind that much. It's trite, but I knew if I did it as well as I could, I would win. If I did it as well as I could, it would have been better than anybody else did it, and therefore I would win."

—**Mickey Wright**, *Thirteen-time Major Champion*

"I feel like I improved off of last week, it's just not really showing itself right now… It feels pretty good. Not great, but good enough to be able to compete." (2020 Wyndham Championship)

—**Jordan Spieth**, *Three-time Major Champion*

Key Principles

1. Little successes add up to big wins.
2. Win or lose, you can always learn from your performance.
3. The only loss is when you don't learn.

Sweet Victory!

Congratulations! You just won a grueling hard-fought tournament! You are drenched, tired, and in need of fluids. Once you've taken care of your physical recuperation it is time to think about the mental side of the equation. Specifically, what do you do now? How can you build on the success you had? Better yet what aspects of your game could you improve? Too often after winning a tournament players get satisfied with the victory and simply move on to the next tournament without evaluating their successful results. This is not the time to rest on your laurels but to stay grounded, humble, continue to improve, build on what is working, and analyze what's not working.

Many coaches like to say that you learn more from your losses than from your wins. Certainly, this can be true of losses as they stand out and hurt more, which in turn forces you to understand where things did not go according to plan. However, do not be fooled as there is important information to be gained from both a loss and a win. Remember that winning or losing is out of your control. Hence, the smart golfer goes beyond the results and looks to improve no matter the outcome.

Whether a golfer wins or loses, they should always ask themselves some key questions about their performance. The goal of asking questions is to raise awareness of what happened.

This workout will highlight seven key questions that golfers should ask themselves after a sweet win or a tough loss.

1. Briefly describe the score and conditions of your round.

This is a simple question for the player to log the score and write down their overall impressions of a round. It might be as simple as, "I shot a -3 with five birdies, but the greens ran very fast and two three-putt greens cost me two bogeys. I played a solid front nine, and then dropped my intensity to start off the back nine. However, I was able to pick it up again for the final five holes." This question is not to be judgmental, but simply to note the objective facts about the competition.

2. How did I feel mentally and physically coming into the tournament?

It's important to check in and understand how you felt in order to assess where you need to go. Oftentimes a golfer might be coming off a big win and is mentally and physically tired. They might be coming off an injury or there is an off-course personal issue that is challenging to them. All these factors influence how you prepare and play so they should be noted. Understanding these issues will help a golfer and coach be aware of the situation and make changes if necessary. After winning the 2021 Sony Open in Hawaii, Keven Na said "I'm so happy at home…and I think that's showing up on the golf course and I thinks that's been the key."

3. What are three things I did well?

It is important to identify our strengths and winning swing thoughts in competition, so we can continue to use and build on them. This awareness will provide feedback to continue building on strengths. There is usually no such thing as a perfect performance and likewise there is also no such thing as a completely flawed performance. It is always somewhere in between. Certainly, we all have our weaknesses—however, our job in competition is to create a situation where we put ourselves in a position to play the shots we want in the situations we want. If we can play to our strengths we have the best chance to compete and subsequently win.

4. What are three things which I can improve on?

Again, if you won, Congratulations. If you lost? Hang in there! There are always areas to further develop and improve. Look at Tiger Woods, he changed the mechanics of his swing multiple times over the course of his career to get better and better. He changed his swing to adapt to his body maturing and adapted for his multiple injuries. Apply such wisdom to your own game by noting weaknesses and how to improve them. Then ask yourself how can I implement these improvements during my off weeks in order to "game" them in my next tournament?

5. If I played in the same pairing or course again, what would I do the same and what would I do differently?

Each course is unique in its own way, understanding the challenges and where you can be more aggressive is important. Again, Kevin Na in his win at the 2021 Sony Open in Hawaii recently shared that he made some mistakes on the front nine but knew if he stayed calm on the back nine he would have some easier holes where he could pick up ground.

6. What are my next steps? Who can help me?

This is an important question as it makes the golfer think about what they need to do next and subsequently who could help them get to the next level. It might be a short-term answer to help them prepare for the next tournament or a longer-term one to help them prepare for the next level in their development. Do you seek out a putting coach or short game coach? Perhaps you seek a sports psychologist or a personal trainer.

7. How do I feel about my effort and play during my round?

Again, this question is a check-in question. It's an opportunity for the golfer to simply identify where they are mentally and physically. An answer might be, "I'm exhausted, but feel good about my effort and I am confident going into the final day tomorrow."

Sweet Victory!

Seven Questions to Ask After Your Round

"Your round doesn't end after the last hole…that's actually the time to evaluate what happened, what you might do differently, and how you can improve next time."

—Rob Polishook

Date:

Golf Course/Weather: _____

1. Describe your round: _____

_____

_____

_____

_____

2. How did I feel mentally and physically coming into the round? _____

_____

_____

_____

3. What are three things I did well?_____

1. _____

2. _____

3. _____

4. What are three things I didn't do well that I can improve on?_____

1. _____

2. _____

3. _____

5. In the next round, what would I do the same? What would I do differently? ____

_____

_____

_____

_____

6. What are my next steps to making these adjustments? Who can help me? _____

_____

_____

_____

_____

7. How did I feel about my effort and play regarding my round? _____

_____

_____

_____

_____

Workout 31
Mental Point

We encounter setbacks, what really determines our strength is how we respond to them.

Fight, Flight, Freeze
The Seven Biggest Fears that Paralyze Golfers

What the Pros Are Saying

"…there were times I didn't even want my putter. I wasn't hyperventilating, but I definitely was not feeling real good coming to the green. It was like Fear Factor. It wasn't a pretty situation."

—**Mark O`Meara**, *Two-time Major Champion*

"I should have turned to them both (caddie and coach, 1996 Masters) and just purged… It would have taken 10 minutes, and it would have been over with. But I didn't do it. So, the lesson there is, don't harbor things internally. Don't push the elephant under the rug. Anxiety and happiness both come from within. And so, you have to ask, which one do you prefer?"

—**Greg Norman**, *Two-time Major Champion*

Key Principles

1. The athlete is a person first and a performer second.
2. Choking happens!
3. Our biggest fears usually come out when we feel most vulnerable.

Fight, Flight, Freeze

How many times have you heard the following from a coach, parent, or significant other: "If only he/she played to their potential…" "If only he/she could play tournaments like he/she plays in practice…" "If only he/she would just let herself go and swing…" We all know the mental side of golf is critically important. Dr. Alan Goldberg, noted sports psychology consultant, stated, "in sports, the mental game is like the glue—it's what holds everything together."

Golf is made up of four parts: technical, strategic, physical, and mental. One of these parts without the others is essentially worthless. Think of your car. The technical part is the body—a stable foundation streamlined to make the car travel smoothly. The strategic part is the steering wheel—able to travel in the desired direction or change course whenever necessary. The physical part is the gas—physical preparation and stamina, the component ensuring that the car has the fuel to complete the journey. The mental part is the engine—the most essential component—the force that starts the car and makes it run. When the four parts are synchronized, our golf game runs like a fine-tuned sports car. Yet, when one of the parts goes awry the car does not run smoothly.

The key question becomes: What gets in the way of a golfer performing well in pressure situations? More often than not it is a result of fears which block the path towards potential unlimited performance. The golfer is aware of these fears but does not accept them, which only creates an internal struggle. Other times the fears may be just below a golfer's conscious thought patterns, and in this case, it becomes necessary to delve a bit deeper into what is actually behind the fears.

Here are seven of the biggest fears that can hold an athlete back from achieving their potential unlimited performance.

1. Fear of Not Being Good Enough

This fear rears its head all the time, both on and off the course; in fact, just thinking about it may trigger an "Aha" moment. We all want to believe in ourselves and feel that we have the ability to be successful, yet anything short of that can be disheartening. In tournament play, golfers get discouraged and begin to fear that they are not good enough to compete with the field; they then lose their will and compete less than 100%. Sometimes in life, and golf, setbacks may seem like a validation of not being good enough—that we lacked what it took to achieve our goal(s). However, while we may have setbacks, what really determines our strength is how we respond to them.

2. Fear of Failure

This fear usually rears its head during a close round especially when a golfer is perceived as being better than their opponents. The seemingly lesser player plays without expectations, but the favored golfer seems to be playing with a weight around their neck. The favored player is afraid to fail because they tie their identity and self-worth into their performance. Additionally, they may be afraid of what others think if they perform below expectations. When a golfer is afraid to experiment, afraid to try new techniques, or afraid to take a risk, their fear of failure is usually the cause.

3. Fear of the Unknown

This fear often rears its head in preparation for a big tournament. This "fear of the unknown" creates a high level of anxiety about what is going to happen. The fear of not being in control of your club face at impact also surfaces. The fear can start on the range. For instance, you don't feel like you can squarely hit the ball with any club and now you have to tee off in minutes. Nobody wants to be the one holding up their group due to errant shots. The feeling of completely losing your swing is a real fear. This is evidenced when one poorly hit shot can lead to rushed swings, poor strategic decisions, and ultimately round-breaking double and triple bogeys. Being aware of one's situation will allow one to play their game and eventually stick to their normal course management.

4. Fear of Being Judged

This often comes up when a golfer is thinking about what their parents, coach, or significant other are thinking as they are playing. This simple mind shift takes the golfer away from their present situation on the course towards something off the course that they can't control. Unconditional acceptance from the support team is so important. When such support is provided the golfer can feel calm, relaxed and safe. Thus, the golfer can play free without any worry of the results.

5. Fear of Not Meeting Expectations

This is similar to the fear of being judged in that the golfer cannot control what someone else expects. Often the expectations of parents, coaches, caddies, and friends are solely focused on your results. The process (the journey) is ignored. For a golfer to play their best, they must be in the present and focus on the experience. Focusing on expectations of results creates a mental distraction.

6. Fear of Success

This fear manifests itself when a golfer has a lead and then begins to think things like, "I shouldn't be beating this person—they are ranked higher than me." Or, this golfer may not view him or herself at a certain skill level and therefore feels undeserving of a victory. Other times, the uncertainty and subsequent anxiety of putting themselves on the line for a possible victory is too much to handle. The certainty of losing, while disappointing, is well-known and a familiar road already traveled.

7. Fear of Injury or Re-Injury

This fear is driven by our macho sports culture's unwillingness to deal with the emotional stress and traumatic experiences that may result from injuries. Specifically neglected is the athlete's uncertainty about recovery, alienation from their support team, fear of not being able to return at full strength, and even anxiety about what might happen should the situation recur. It is important to note that while the athlete may be cleared physically by doctors, emotionally they still may not have processed through the fear. Anyone who has experienced an injury understands how the mental scars do not just disappear when the doctor says you're cleared to play.

In today's sporting society, exhibiting any sign of weakness or fear is difficult for a player. Society views vulnerability as weakness, whereas in reality, awareness of vulnerability equates to true strength. Fears like the seven mentioned above creep up all the time! Especially in pressure situations that often lead to fight, flight, or freeze states. Yet, recognizing such fears and having the awareness, curiosity, resiliency, and support system to help work through them is what truly enables us to grow and reach our individual potential.

Sometimes when things are *falling apart* they may actually be falling into place

Fight, Flight, Freeze

The Seven Biggest Fears That Paralyze Athletes

Rate these fears in order of how they affect you:

	Fear of not being good enough		Fear of not meeting expectations
	Fear of failure		Fear of success
	Fear of the unknown		Fear of injury/re-injury
	Fear of being judged		Other (did I miss one? Shanking)

Choose the top fear and write it here: _____

When you think of this fear, what do you experience? _____

_____

What is the scariest aspect about that fear? _____

On a scale of 1 to 10 (10 being the most), how strong is the fear? _____

How do you experience the fear on the course (i.e. tight/restricting)? _____

_____

Where do you feel the fear in your body? _____

Now, bring your attention to a time on the course when you felt calm. How did you experience it? _____

_____

Where do you feel the calm in your body? _____

Now, take a minute to notice the calm. Go back to noticing the fear...how do you experience it now? _____

_____

Usually the fear will subside.

Workout 32
Mental Point

We often forget that behind the superstar athlete's exterior, the athlete is a person first and performer second.

I Can't Believe I Choked!
Understanding Slumps, Blocks and the Yips

What the Pros Are Saying

"The athlete's mind and body always hold the answers."

> —**Drs. Grand and Goldberg**, This Is Your Brain on Sports

"We believe that one should never separate an athlete's performance problem from who he or she is as a unique human being."

> —**Drs. Grand and Goldberg**, This Is Your Brain on Sports

"The unconscious accumulation of physical and emotional traumas in the athlete's brain and body are the root causes of all significant performance problems."

> —**Drs. Grand and Goldberg**, This Is Your Brain on Sports

Key Principles

1. When a golfer walks onto the course, their experiences, fears, and traumas follow them.
2. Trust yourself, trust your game.

I Can't Believe I Choked!

How many times have you seen a golfer get tight, underperform, or choke in a big tournament? In practice, they play great with not a care in the world while going for broke on every shot and effortlessly succeeding while doing so. Yet once the tournament starts their favorite clubs become their worst. Their normal accuracy off the tee results in pulled hooks into the deep rough. Inexplicably, one´s reliable long iron game suddenly falters as you hit into trap after trap. Getting up and down with your short game loses its effectiveness. Or maybe the formerly simple act of a three-foot par saving putt now becomes unmanageable. Fans become dumbfounded and cannot believe that an elite athlete can succumb to this type of pressure. "How can this happen? What's the cause of this?"

In looking for the solution, many coaches, fans, players, media, and even performance experts start by critiquing what they can see (i.e. the sliced drives, or three-putting). Their initial focus is to look above the surface to find what is broken in hopes of a technical "quick fix." Certainly, this can be a place to look if the situation occurs once or twice. However, if the choke or slump continues repeatedly under pressure, it falls in the category of a repetitive sports performance block.

A repetitive sports performance block (i.e. choke, slump, yips) is actually the *symptom* of an underlying issue. The *cause* is an accumulation of negative experiences from which the golfer has not been able to move on from. In actuality, this block has little to do with the last time the golfer "choked." Rather, something about that pressure situation was the trigger that brought the unprocessed issue or issues to the surface where it distracted the golfer's performance. In fact, before or during a tournament, some golfers are aware that "something is just not right." They experience underlying nervousness and anxiety and try to hide or resist it. Oftentimes, the golfer doesn't want to address their anxiety for fear of being judged by teammates or fans as lacking mental toughness. Yet other times, the golfer may be completely unaware of the root cause of their anxiety since it has been disassociated from their consciousness in an effort to protect their personal psyche. Either way the golfer's performance bears the burden.

Much like "heavy baggage" we hold onto on a daily basis, these negative experiences can grip a person and accumulate during a person's life from both on and off the course incidents. Emotional trauma can come from situations such as embarrassment from slicing into the trees, overshooting the green on a short chip or repeatedly missing short, par-saving putts. Physical trauma can derive from writhing in lower back pain after over-rotating on a tee shot or simply rolling one's ankle climbing out of a sand trap. Additionally, off-course trauma can occur and accumulate stemming from issues such as divorce, death, car accidents, or other circumstances. Similarly, excessive judgment, expectations, and opponent comparisons from parents, coaches, caddies, media, or friends can also unknowingly add weight to the burden of pressure and distract a golfer from playing freely.

Throughout our lives we encounter physical and emotional trauma. Depending upon the severity of these instances and our preparedness to meet them at the time we successfully absorb and process through these encounters while other times we do not. When we are unable to process these experiences, the stress does not evaporate over time. Rather, we store the unprocessed memory in the brain and body where it may show itself at unexpected times. During the intense pressure of a round a golfer's psyche may recall a similar error from their previous tournament that they tense up, hesitate, or even freeze mid-swing. During the 2016 Masters final round Spieth´s tee shot to the 12th hole was not the first time he landed in Rae´s Creek. The same pressure situation occurred in the 2014 Masters final round with a poor tee shot into Rae´s Creek while down one stroke to Bubba Watson.

These unprocessed negative experiences can accumulate like balls in a bucket. Imagine that each individual issue represents a ball. Some may carry the weight of a single golf ball while other issues are bigger like a sleeve of golf balls, and even bigger issues like two sleeves of balls—depending upon the level of stress and anxiety the golfer carries. These emotional/physical trauma-like experiences get held in the body's central nervous system. They directly interfere with the golfer's ability to access and adapt to situations and perform movements that were once so easy and instinctual. Finally, as experiences accumulate, a ball tumbles out of the bucket. It is at this moment the golfer's repetitive sports performance block is now on public display for all to see, judge, and evaluate. When in reality, the ball that fell was metaphorically the straw that broke the camel's back!

We often forget that behind the superstar athlete's exterior, the athlete is a person first and a performer second. They are a whole human athlete. It is almost impossible not to be affected by the troubling day-to-day issues which we all experience. Each person holds on to different things in different ways.

In summary, it's clear that we hold emotional (fears) and physical (injuries) trauma-like experiences in our bodies. As a person this "baggage" can consciously or unconsciously affect how we react, adapt, and adjust to everyday situations. As a golfer, it can also carry onto the course and affect an athlete's ability to perform; especially in a high-pressure situation.

I Can't Believe I Choked!

Think of a time you choked or got really uptight...when was it? Where was it? Who were you playing with?

_____

_____

_____

What did you try to do at the time to try and manage the situation?

_____

_____

_____

Describe in detail what happened, and what you experienced...

Before: _____

_____

_____

During: _____

_____

_____

After: _____

_____

_____

Has it happened in another area of your life, on or off the course? Describe it.

_____

_____

_____

_____

_____

Recognizing the above, what does this make you aware of?

_____

_____

_____

What are three things you could try next time as you feel yourself starting to get tense?

1. _____

2. _____

3. _____

Conclusion

What's Next?

Golf Inside the Zone is intended to stimulate ideas, thoughts, and questions. Ultimately the workbook is intended to provide a foundation to help you become more self-aware, curious, and to embrace competition over the course of your athletic journey. Like any journey different events and experiences will bring different insights—be aware of these insights and continually build on them.

Golf Inside the Zone is meant to continually evolve and bring you back to a centered place, no matter where you are on your competitive journey. Because of this, I encourage you to revisit and reassess the workouts throughout your journey. In my experience, any path to improvement is one step at a time. This process must be encountered with patience, purpose, and perseverance, both for others and for yourself. This reminds me of the Chinese proverb, "a journey of a thousand miles starts with a single step."

Now that you have read and experienced *Golf Inside the Zone*, I thank you for your time and hope you have found it both rewarding and thought-provoking. Please share with me your insights, experiences, successes, failures and obstacles. I genuinely look forward to reconnecting with you in my future books, workshops, or consultations.

My Next Step...

As I mentioned, like your personal journey, mine is also evolving. In the Introduction I mentioned how this book started with my clients asking me questions related to mental training. Little did I know at the time that it would eventually lead to me publishing my third book!

But as we know, no journey is complete without the next step...My next step is to choose certain key chapters and expand on them in another book. With this in mind, I have already begun writing a book called *The Whole Human Athlete: The Journey Beyond the Score*. After that, I will write: *Doggedness: Mental Skills Athletes Can Learn from Animals*. Stay tuned, the best is yet to come

B'simcha (with happiness)

Rob

P.S. If you want to chat more, share an idea, experience, or thought, agree or disagree with something I said, please contact me at:

rob@insidethezone.com
www.insidethezone.com
973-723-0314

I'll look forward to hearing from you!

Biography of the Author

Rob Polishook, M.A., C.P.C., is the founder and director of Inside the Zone Sports Performance Group, LLC. As a mental training coach, he works with athletes and teams from junior players to professionals, helping them to uncover their mental edge—often the difference between winning and losing. He specializes in helping athletes overcome performance blocks (i.e. yips, chokes, slumps, anxiety), helping athletes work through the "unspoken" psychological trauma from injuries, helping already high-performing athletes reach beyond self-imposed barriers, and teaching innovative mental training skills, tools, and techniques.

Rob's non-judgmental manner encourages athletes to work with performance issues using awareness, acceptance, and brain/body intuition. This unique inside-out approach encourages empowerment and trust in self and the process. Rob's focus is on the athlete as a person first and a performer second which he coined Whole Human Athlete. Through this lens he recognizes that day-to-day, on and off-the-course experiences directly impact how an athlete performs especially under pressure.

Rob has presented workshops in India, Israel and the United States. He regularly runs week-long workshops called "Unleashing the Performer Within" at the highly acclaimed Omega Institute. Additionally, his articles have been published nationally and internationally and he has been quoted in *Sports Illustrated*. He has also been featured in interviews with ESPN radio.

Rob has earned a Masters degree in psychological studies with a concentration in sport and exercise psychology from Seton Hall University (SHU) and has completed his certification in sport psychology from SHU. He is a certified professional/life coach from IPEC, an international federation coaching affiliate. He has also received certifications in Somatic Experiencing, Brainspotting Sports Performance Work, Focusing and Jim Loehr's Mental Toughness Program. Additionally, he is a certified Mindfulness teacher and incorporates spirituality and animal wisdom into his teachings.

Rob and his wife Debbie live in New York City. He can often be spotted walking his dog Gumbo in Central park and/or having coffee with his wife Debbie at a neighborhood coffee shop.

Founded in 2005, Inside the Zone Sports Performance Group was born from Rob Polishook's passion for sports, his love of working with kids, and his curiosity in understanding the process of what it takes to help athletes break beyond obstacles, challenges and barriers. The goal of Inside the Zone Sports Performance Group is to assist golfers, at all levels, to uncover their mental edge and unleash their unlimited peak performance.

The mental side plays a large role in golf and any sport. It is remiss that the real mental issues regarding competition, focus, goals, nerves, and the athlete as a person first are not being addressed. These issues include but are not limited to:

- Competing under pressure
- Dealing with adversity and using the experience to learn and bounce back
- Handling pressure and expectations
- Concentrating under pressure
- Staying centered, balanced and calm
- Focusing on the process and not on the leaderboard
- Crafting strategies for goal setting
- Reaching beyond self imposed barriers

Inside the Zone Sports Performance Group services:

- One-on-one and group consultations for athletes, parents, and coaches
- Workshops and seminars for teams, parents, and coaches
- Dynamic season-long consultations for teams

Rob Polishook, M.A., C.P.C. Mental Training Coach

www.insidethezone.com
@insidethezone.com
rob@insidethezone.com

Whole Human Athlete™
Heart . Energy . Spirit

About Rob: *The Back Story*

Who am I?

I was born imperfect—or maybe perfectly imperfect! Here's a great example from my first grade class trip: All I remember is spinning around a revolving door at the Empire State Building, getting my shoe caught and holding up everyone from access to the door for three minutes while being laughed at by my class. Once we were back in the classroom, I was unable to read. The letters were a jumbled mess, teachers would get frustrated, and I was ashamed to raise my hand. I was diagnosed with a form of dyslexia and a motor learning problem.

I vividly remember being left behind in first grade and attempting to explain the reason to my friends. Even clearer was my memory of getting special tutoring from Mrs. Schaffer after school on reading, writing and arithmetic. Going into third grade I couldn't read or write cursive and this presented a problem. It felt like I was in a foreign country. The only place I might have felt normal was Hebrew school but here I didn't understand the Hebrew letters and the fact that you read right to left. In my spare time, I remember balancing on a board, the kind with a roller underneath, which was supposed to help with my coordination and balance.

I did these types of exercises my entire childhood! Extra work was something that was part of my upbringing. I never had time to feel sorry for myself or ask

why I was different; I just went to the extra tutoring and got on my balance board for hours.

I learned at an early age never, never, never to give up. I never let an opportunity for extra credit pass by. And I never stopped training at anything I cared about.

I was lucky. At an early age I experienced what it was like to have a strong support system, with parents who believed in me. Because of my learning disabilities, I learned to be empathetic to others who didn't get things done as fast or as well as the rest of the class.

Why am I writing this book?

Every day I listen to athletes tell me about their fears, anxieties, and performance blocks. I hear how they stand frozen over a 3 foot putt or how they constantly get caught in a negative spiral during pressure situations. It reminds me of how when I was a kid, I wished I had someone I could open up to and let them know how I was feeling and experience a situation from my point of view. Instead, my coaches always told me how I was supposed to be feeling and what I could or couldn't do. If nothing else, a book like this would have been valuable just to have an outlet to let go, and in some cases verify what I was thinking was "normal."

After I listen to what my clients are saying I usually express to them that they are not alone in what they are thinking and feeling. In fact, their thinking and feelings are often shared by many athletes in the same situation on all levels. This reassurance usually makes them feel like a 500-pound weight has been lifted off their shoulders. When I tell them that they are not broken and they don't need fixing, that the answers lie within, and that we just need to uncover them, they usually take a big sigh and exhale in relief.

Rob, Debbie, and Gumbo

Acknowledgments

A book like this doesn't happen without the support and encouragement from many people.

First, and foremost I'd like to thank my dear friend John Martini, whom I initially met 25 years ago on the tennis court as I wore my #23 Michael Jordan basketball jersey! John has been a steadfast friend and student of the mental side of golf, history and playing the game itself. John has taught me so much about golf, it's intricacies and beauty. Alas, John was present as he witnessed my 150 yard skulled 7 iron that somehow rolled in for an eagle in Las Vegas. Possibly the ugliest shot in the world only rivaled by my other mishits but John reminded me that all that matters is that the ball went in! John can be found on his local course in Uruguay working on his game, teaching his daughter Madison the game, and sharing swing thoughts with the local pros. Simply put, this book doesn't happen without John's knowledge, encouragement, and what we call the sniff test for authenticity.

Next up is John Baum, a graduate student in my Seton Hall graduate class. John's curiosity, focus, and drive is what initially clued me in that this guy is passionate about golf, sports and the mental side. John was instrumental in the development of all the golf workouts. His work with kids is inspirational and he has a bright future in the field.

Thanks to Ivy Vinnick, her reliability and attention to detail helped keep *Golf Inside the Zone* moving forward. Thanks to Ryan Silwak, now finishing up his Ph.D. at Seton Hall and doing great work in the mental health field.

Thanks to Kellie Patterson, she continues to be instrumental in the graphic development of *Inside the Zone* projects. Thanks to John Reinhardt, who has been a guiding light in *Golf Inside the Zone's* book format.

Thanks to Dr. Alan Goldberg a great mentor and long-time friend. He was always encouraging and teaching me especially the foundational idea that an athlete is a person first and a performer second!

Thanks to Dr. Sandra Lee, Dr. Riley Nickols, Dr. Jerry Lynch, Ian Halperin who have always been supportive and encouraging of my work. Thanks to Michael Buttacavoli, Mariano Bartolome and David Armitage and all of my golf clients and clients in all sports. You know who you are!

Thanks to my Dad, Shimshon, and my Mum, Jean: her devotion to inspire others lives inside of me.

Big hug and thanks to my bride of 33 years, Debbie. None of this work could ever have begun without your unconditional love, support, and belief in me. You listen to all my crazy ideas and encourage me to pursue most of them! You have been my rock of stability. Finally, thanks to Gumbo, as she patiently sits in my office as I work.

Tiger's Sunday red

Quote Sources by Workout

Workout 1

Evers, D. (2020). "18 Great Mental Tips." https://www.golfdigest.com/gallery/golf-mental-quotes.

Pages, J. (2016). "The return of golf's almost-greatest." https://www.sunstar.com.ph/article/112986/Pages-The-return-of-golfs-almost-greatest.

Chicago Golf Lessons. (2016). "The Power of Positivity in Golf." http://www.mychicagogolflesson.com/golf-blog/2016/3/13/the-power-of#:~:text=There%20are%20numerous%20quotes%20relating,the%20distance%20between%20your%20ears.%22.

Golf Compendium. (2019) "Walter Hagen Quotes." https://www.golfcompendium.com/2019/01/walter-hagen-quotes.html.

Workout 2

GolfWRX Staff. (2019). The Gear Dive: Coaches Edition: Adam Schriber. http://www.golfwrx.com/567032/the-gear-dive-coaches-edition-adam-schriber/.

GolfWRX Staff. (2019). The Gear Dive: Matthew Wolff's swing coach George Gankas. http://www.golfwrx.com/565168/the-gear-dive-matthew-wolffs-swing-coach-george-gankas/.

Griffin, L. (2020). "The Hill." https://www.theplayerstribune.com/en-us/articles/the-hill-lanto-griffin-golf.

Grand, D. personal communication.

Koepka, B. (2020). *Michael Collin's America's Caddie*. Season 1, Episode 1.

Tomlinson, S. (2020) *12 Golf Quotes to Lift Us Up*. https://firsttee.org/2020/04/16/12-golf-quotes-to-lift-us-up/?gclid=EAIaIQobChMI2JH8vOfw6gIVCorICh1e-wtBEAAYASAAEgJsC_D_BwE.

Workout 3

Helm, B. (2015). *5 Life Lessons from GoDaddy's Bob Parsons*. https://www.inc.com/burt-helm/bob-parsons-iconic.html.

Ferguson, D. (2012). "MASTERS: Bubba Watson defeats Louis Oosthuizen in playoff." https://www.nhregister.com/news/article/MASTERS-Bubba-Watson-defeats-Louis-Oosthuizen-in-11542748.php.

Beshore B. (2012) "Golf the Game of Life." https://www.forbes.com/sites/brentbeshore/2012/08/20/golf-the-game-of-life/#108f5a04bcf8

Gains, C. (2019). "20 of Arnold Palmer's Greatest Quotes." https://www.businessinsider.com/arnold-palmer-quotes-2016-9

Heath, E. (2020). "10 of the Best Arnold Palmer Quotes." https://www.golf-monthly.co.uk/features/the-game/10-best-arnold-palmer-quotes-152590

Alpine Golf Club (2019) "9 Inspirational Jack Nicklaus Quotes." http://www.alpinegolf-club.com/news_and_events/9-inspirational-jack-nicklaus-quotes-every-golfer-must-read/#:~:text=%E2%80%9CResolve%20never%20to%20quit%2C%20never,no%20matter%20what%20the%20situation.%E2%80%9D&text=%E2%80%9CFocus%20on%20remedies%20not%20faults.%E2%80%9D&text=%E2%80%9CA%20kid%20grows%20up%20a,teaches%20you%20how%20to%20behave.%E2%80%9D

Workout 4

Weinman, S. (2016). "The Shark's Collapse." https://www.golfdigest.com/story/the-sharks-collapse-20-years-later.

Ferguson, D. (2012). "MASTERS: Bubba Watson defeats Louis Oosthuizen in playoff." https://www.nhregister.com/news/article/MASTERS-Bubba-Watson-defeats-Louis-Oosthuizen-in-11542748.php

Shipnuck, A. (2019). "The more unbelievable story in golf: A treacherous border crossing was just the beginning of Jose de Jesus Rodriguez's journey to the PGA tour." https://golf.com/news/news-features/2019/01/08/jose-de-jesus-rodriguez-long-hard-journey-to-the-pgatour/?utmsource=The+Fried+Egg+Golf+Newsletter&utm_campaign=497315621c-EMAIL_CAMPAIGN_2019_01_09_04_56&utm_medium=email&utm_term=0_28a08c87c2-4973156

Dethier, Dylan. (2020). "Why Bryson DeChambeau changed his game plan at the PGA Championship." https://golf.com/news/bryson-dechambeau-changed-pga-game-plan/

Workout 5

Crouse, K. (2019). "Chasing for Years, Ernie Els Has Tiger Woods Right Where He Wants Him." https://www.nytimes.com/2019/12/13/sports/golf/ernie-els-tiger-woods-presidents-cup.html.

Shipnuck, A. (2019). "The more unbelievable story in golf: A treacherous border crossing was just the beginning of Jose de Jesus Rodriguez's journey to the PGA tour." https://golf.com/news/jose-de-jesus-rodriguez-long-hard-journey-to-the-pga-tour/#:~:text=News-,The%20most%20unbelievable%20story%20in%20golf'%3A%20A%20treacherous%20border,journey%20to%20the%20PGA%20Tour&text=%E2%80%9CEl%20Camar%C3%B3n%2C%E2%80%9D%20as%20

Rodr%C3%ADguez,sure%20that%20I%20would%20die.%22&text=Salvation%20
beckoned%20on%20the%20other%20side%20of%20the%20river.

Sorenstam, A. [@ANNIKA59]. (2019, July 22.) Annika Foundation Tweet.

Ramathan, N. (2008). "Open Mic: Yes, Golf is a Sport." https://bleacherreport.com/
acticles/31705-open-mic-yes-golf-is-a-sport.

Press Conference, The Masters Press Room. (2015). "Jordan Spieth, Masters Champion,
Speaks. Addresses the Media on Sunday." http://www.jordanspiethgolf.com/article/
jordan-spieth-masters-champion-speaks-addresses-the-media-on-sunday.

Workout 6.

Heath, E. (2020). "Jon Rahm Wins the Memorial to Become
Number One." https://www.golf-montly.co.uk/news/tour-news/
jon-rahm-wins-the-memorial-to-become-world-number-one-201895.

Scotty Cameron Putters. (2020). "Inside the Circle T with Brad Faxon (Part 1)." https://
www.youtube.com/watch?v=N0_SWMYpDXs.

Pennington, B. (2020). "De Chambeau's Latest Physics Experiment? Himself?" https://
www.nytimes.com/2020/06/24/sports/golf/bryson-dechambeau- weight.html?refer
ringSource=articleShare.

Heath, E. (2020). "10 of the Best Arnold Palmer Quotes." https://www.golf-monthly.
co.uk/features/the-game/10-best-arnold-palmer-quotes-152590.

Oscarson, P. (2013). "10 Quotes to Help You in Golf (and Life)." https://bleacherreport.
com/articles/1763026-10-quotes-to-help-you-in-golf-and-life

Goldberg, personal communication, August, 18, 2020.

Workout 7

Gray, W. (2020). "Mathew Wolff (64) snaps out of slump and now seeks second title."
https://www.golfchannel.com/news/matthew-wolff-64-snaps-out-slump-and-now-
seeks-second-title. https://coloradoavidgolfer.com/50-best-golf-quotes-of-all-time/.

DiMeglio, S. (2020). "Woodland's U.S. Open reign continues, expending time
to reflect on biggest win." https://golfweek.usatoday.com/2020/06/18/
gary-woodland-u-s-open-reign-continues/.

Park, R. (2013). *50 Best Golf Quotes of All-Time*.

Townsand, C. (1999). *Golf Champions Motivational Quotes*. https://www.mindtraining-
forgolf.com/golf-champion-quotes.php.

DiMeglio, S. (2020). "Justin Thomas is going to 'hurt for a while' after painful Workday loss." https://golfweek.usatoday.com/2020/07/12/
justin-thomas-pga-tour-hurt-painful-workday-loss/.

Golf Channel Digital. (2013). They Said it: "Best Quotes from Master's Friday." https://www.golfchannel.com/news/they-said-it-best-quotes-masters-friday.

Workout 8

Snead, S. (n.d.). *Sam Snead Biography*. https://www.worldgolfhalloffame.org/sam-snead/.

Tappin, N. (2020). Dustin Johnson Exclusive—"I'd like To Get A Few More Majors." https://www.golf-monthly.co.uk/features/the-game/dustin-johnson-exclusive-id-like-to-get-a-few-more-majors-202251.

Mackenzie, D. (n.d.). "The 5 Biggest Mental Mistakes in Golf." Audio podcast episode. https://golfstateofmind.com/overcome-5-biggest-mental-mistakes-golf-email/.

Redford, R. (2000). *The Legend of Bagger Vance*.

Bolt, T. (2020). "21 Inspirational Golf Quotes." https://wwwgolfdigest.com/gallery/21-inspirational-golf-quotes.

Workout 9

Lesson Tee. (2010). *Golf Digest*. https://www.golfdigest.com/story/flick-nicklaus-film.

MacKenzie, D. (2015). "Visualization in Golf." https://golfstateofmind.com/powerful-visualization-golf/.

Harig, B. (2020). "Reinvigorated by return, Martin Kaymer shoots 66 at PGA Championship." https://www.espn.com/golf/story/_/id/29610450/reinvigorated-return-martin-kaymer-shoots-66-pga-championship.

Menta, N. (2019). "Woods Hasn't Come to Grips with his Masters Win." https://www.golfchannel.com/news/tiger-woods-says-he-hasnt-come-grips-his-2019-masters-win.

Workout 10

Boren, C. (2016). "Tiger Woods says he's 'nervous' about golfing again, but 'I'm not dead'". https://www.washingtonpost.com/news/early-lead/wp/2016/11/28/tiger-woods-says-hes-nervous-about-golfing-again-but-im-not-dead/.

Holmes, A. (2014). Impact: "Harry Vardon did pretty much everything in golf including set fashion trends." https://www.golfdigest.com/content/golfdigest-com/en/the-loop/_default/article/2014/5/impact-harry-vardon-did-just-a.html.

Nicholas, J. (2015). "4 Ways to Reduce Public Speaking Anxiety." https://medium.com/@jeremienicholas/4-ways-to-reduce-public-speaking-anxiety-c13bf51c2b6a.

Pennington, B. (2016). "To Calm his Jittery Nerves, Keegan Bradley Embraces Them." https://www.nytimes.com/2016/07/16/sports/golf/keegan-bradley-british-open.html

Workout 11

Barret, D. (n.d.). "NA NA NA NA…HEY HEY, GOODBYE IS THE TREND FOR 54-HOLE LEADERS." http://theaposition.com/davidhbarrett/silos/pga-tour/1658/
na-na-na-nahey-hey-goodbye-is-the-trend-for-54-hole-leaders.

Chronicles Unseen. (2020). "Jack Nicklaus: Adaptability is the key to Golden Open Run."
https://www.theopen.com/Latest/Jack-Nicklaus-Chronicles-Unseen.

Penick, Harvey (1992) (Little red book) *Harvey Penick´s Little Red Book: Lessons and Teachings from a Lifetime in Golf*/Harvey Penick with Bud Shrake, Simon & Shuster, Inc. page 45.

Schupak, A. (2020) "Breathe In, Breathe Out: Bubba Watson hires breathing coach, shoots 65 at Northern Trust". https://golfweek.usatoday.com/2020/08/20/
bubba-watson-breathing-coach-shoots-65-northern-trust/.

Workout 12

Langer, B. (2019). "Benhard Langer: Built from Bricks." https://www.golfdigest.com/
story/bernhard-langer-built-from-bricks-my-shot-pga-tour-champions.

Piastowski, N. (2020). "Webb Simpson wins the RBC Heritage and three things you should know." https://golf.com/news/webb-simpson-wins-rbc-
heritage-by-one-stroke/.

Cotter, L. (2020). "Lynn on the Links. 65 Best Golf Quotes for Inspiration and Motivation."
https://lynnonthelinks.com/best-golf-quotes-inspiration-motivation/.

Workout 13

Solomon, M. (2020). Golf Channel Television Broadcast. Orlando, FL. NBC Studios.

Kuo, K. (2020). "Jason Kokrak wins star-studded CJ Cup for first
PGA Tour title." https://golfweek.usatoday.com/2020/10/18/
jason-kokrak-claims-cj-cup-at-shadow-creek-for-his-first-pga-tour-win/.

Yocom, G. (2010). "My Shot: Sam Snead." https://www.golfdigest.com/story/
myshot_gd0204.

Schrock, J. (2020). NBC Sports. https://www.nbcsports.com/bayarea/golf/
jordan-spieth-searching-major-magic-hunt-elusive-grand-slam.

Crouse, K. (2019). "When Golf is Nothing but Rough." https://www.nytimes.
com/2019/06/12/sports/us-open-pebble-beach-.html.

Unknown (2012). "Golf is a Mind Game." https://www.golfisamindgame.com/
handling-competition-nerves/.

Workout 14

Crook, J. (2019). "Woodland says U.S. Open-winning game still needs some work." Golf Channel. https://golfchannel.com/news/gary-woodland-says-us-open-winning-game-still-needs-some-work.

Weinman, S. (2016). "The Shark's Collapse." *Golf Digest*. https://golfdigest.com/story/the-sharks-collapse-20-years-later.

ESPN (n.d.). "'Woods' secret weapon is 'cocoon of concentration.'"https://Espn.com/video/clip/_/id/18958555.

Goldberg, Alan, personal communication, August, 18, 2020.

Workout 15

Unknown. (2011). Sport Psychology Quotes. https://sportpsychquotes.wordpress.com/2011/02/19/546/.

MacKenzie, D. (2019). "How To Prepare For A Golf Tournament." https://golfstateofmind.com/how-to-prepare-for-a-golf-tournament/.

Pennington, B. (2020). "I Just Cost Myself 250 Grand." https://www.nytimes.com/2020/07/09/sports/golf/golf-putt-for-dough.html.

Inglis, M. (2016). "Rory McIlroy's Insane Pre-Masters Ritual." https://www.bunkered.co.uk/golf-news/rory-mcilroys-insane-pre-masters-ritual.

Knowlton, E. (2016). "Jason Day Mastered His Mental Game by Adding a 15-Step Visualization Routine Before Every Shot—and Now He's The Best Golfer in The World." https://www.businessinsider.com/jason-day-the-masters-insane-15-step-pre-shot-routine-2016-4.

Workout 16

Babineau, J. 92018). "Howell finds merit in persistence on Tour." https://www.morningread.com/news-opinion/feature/2018-11-20/howell-finds-merit-in-persistence-on0tour.

DiMeglio, S. (2020) "Woodland's U.S. Open reign continues, extending time to reflect on biggest win." https://golfweekusatoday.com/2020/06/18/gary-woodland-u-s-open-reign-continues/.

Workout 17

Nicklaus, J. (2007). *Golf My Way*, p. 213.

Ko, Lydia. https://read.nxtbook.com/global_golf_post/global_golf_post/20210419/lpga_breakout.html?utm_source=newsletter&utm_medium=email&utm_content=READ%20NOW&utm_campaign=dm-041921

Workout 18

Rains, B. (2020). "Drama ahead: Five golfers within four shots of the lead entering Sunday's final round of the Albertsons Boise Open." https://www.idahopress.com/sports/drama-ahead-five-golfers-within-four-shots-of-the-lead-entering-sundays-final-found-of/article_d6b7596d-cabe-5f44-957e-9118b174a9b0.html.

O'Conner, I. (2020). "Phil Mickelson dares Winged Foot's haunting U.S. Open memories once more." https://www.espn.com/golf/story/_/id/29868936/phil-mickelson-dares-winged-foot-haunting-us-open-memories-once-more.

Snead, S. *Sam Snead on Golf*.

Workout 19

Associated Press. (2020). "Michael Thompson wins 3M Open by two strokes." https://www.espon.com/golf/story/_/id/29544556/michael-thompson-wins-3m-open-two-strokes.

Heath, E. (2020). "Zach Johnson Breaks Down After Receiving Payne Stewart Award." https://www.golf-monthly.co.uk/news/tour-news/zach-johnson-breaks-down-after-receiving-payne-stewart-award-203669

Weinman, S. (2016). "The Shark's Collapse." https://www.golfdigest.com/story/the-sharks-collapse-20-years-later

DiMeglio, S. (2020). "Bubba Watson on dealing with anxiety: I thought I was going to die." *Golf Week*. https://golfweek.usatoday.com/2020/10/28/bubba-watson-anxiety-pga-tour/.

McCabe, J. (2016). "Dustin Johnson, reserved and unflappable, but not exempt from nerves." https://golfweek.usatoday.com/2016/09/21/pga-tour-championship-dustin-johnson-nerves/

Roberts, A. (2017). "Jordan Spieth's secret weapon at Open? Chewing Gum." https://www.golfmagic.com/golf-news/jordan-spieths-secret-weapon-open-chewing-gum

Stricklin, A. (2020). "Jack Burke, the oldest living major champ has seen it all—and you can bet he has something to say about it." https://golf.com/news/features/jack-burke-oldest-living-masters-champ

Workout 20

Team Titleist (2020). "Seven Questions with C.T. Pan." https://www.titleist.com/teamtitleist/b/tourblog/posts/seven-questions-with-c-t-pan

Lavner, R. (2014). "Confident Reed: I'm a top-5 player in the world." https://www.golf-channel.com/article/golf-central-blog/confident-reed-im-top-5-player-world

Garcia, S. (2008). "Johnson fires 64 to win Milwaukee." *New York Post*.

O'Connor, I. (2020). "Phil Mickelson dares Winged Foot haunting U.S. Open memories once more." https://www.espn.com/golf/story/_/id/29868936/phil-mickelson-dares-winged-foot-haunting-us-open-memories-once-more

Workout 21

Schlaback, M. (2020). "I'm defending, aren't I? OK just checking'—Why Brooks Koepka never doubts Brooks Koepka." https://www.espn.com/golf/story/_/id/29590738/defending-ok-just-checking-why-brooks-koepka-never-doubts-brooks-koepka

Bleier, R. (2020). "Christina Kim's transformation is positively impacting every part of her life." https://golf.com/news/features/christina-kim-transformation-positive-impact-life/

Barret, D. (n.d.). "NA NA NA NA… HEY HEY, GOODBYE is the trend for 54-hole leaders. "Michael Thompson wins 3M Open." https://www.golf-monthly.co.uk/news/tour-news/michael-thompson-wins-3m-open-202297utm_source=ET&utm_medium=email&utm_campaign=&utm_content=&utm_term=_.

Refresh Leadership, (2019). Leadership lessons from professional golfers. http://www.refreshleadership.com/index.php/2019/04/words-leadership-lessons-professional-golfers/.

Workout 23

Hoggard, R. (2018). "Spieth calm, cool, and in control again at Augusta." https://www.golfchannel.com/news/2018-masters-jordan-spieth-calm-cool-and-control-again-augusta.

Murphy, Michael, (1972,) Penguin Books 1997, Golf in the Kingdom, see shivas.org

Workout 24

Associated Press, (2021). "Sam Burns, 24, Wins Valspar Championship for First PGA Tour Title." https://www.golfdigest.com/story/sam-burns-wins-valspar-championship

Crouse, K. (2018). "Patrick Reed wins the Masters in a breakthrough performance." https://www.nytimes.com/2018/04/08/sports/golf/patrick-reed-masters-.html?action=click&module=RelatedLinks&pgtype=Article/.

Gray, W. (2020). "Matthew Wolff (64) snaps out of slump and now seeks a second title." https://www.golfchannel.com/news/matthew-wolff-64-snaps-out-slump-and-now-seeks-second-title.

Workout 25

Oller, R. "The Memorial: Answers proving elusive for Jordan Spieth after 74 on Saturday." https://golfweek.usatoday.com/2020/07/18/the-memorial-answers-proving-elusive-for-jordan-spieth-after-74-on-saturday/.

Rabionowitz, B. (2020). "With 'Bones' on the bag, Matthew Fitzpatrick has best outing this season." https://golfweek.usatoday.com/2020/07/20/with-bones-on-the-bag-matthew-fitzpatrick-has-best-outing-this-season/.

Unknown, (n.d.). Inbee Park Quotes https://www.brainyquote.com/quotes/inbee_park_631172.

Workout 26

Weinman, S. (2016). "The Shark's Collapse." https://www.golfdigest.com/story/the-sharks-collapse-20-years-later.

Evers, D. (2020). "18 great mental tips." https://www.golfdigest.com/gallery/golf-mental-quotes.

Fields, B. (2019). "Chasing Sam Snead's 82: The PGA tour record Tiger is pursuing has an interesting story of its own." https://www.golfdigest.com/story/chasing-sam-snead-82-the-pga-tour-win-record-tiger-woods-is-pursuing-has-an-interesting-story-of-its-own#:~:text=When%20Snead%20won%20the%20individual,after%20his%20196%205%20%20Greensboro%20triumph.

Workout 27

Crouse, K. (2018). "Patrick Reed wins the Masters in a breakthrough performance." https://www.nytimes.com/2018/04/08/sports/golf/patrick-reed-masters-.html?action=clickmodule=RelatedLinks&pgtype=Article.

Arkush, M. (2019). "Ed Sneed looks back on a near miss." https://www.nytimes.com/2019/04/10/sports/golf/ed-sneed-masters-golf.html.

DiMeglio, S. (2020). "With back against the wall, Harris English becomes Harris English again." https://golfweek.usatoday.com/2020/06/04/with-back-against-the-wall-harris-english-becomes-harris-english-again/.

Workout 28

Panday, S. (2020). "Top 13 Ken Venturi quotes." Players Bio https://playersbio.com/ken-venturi-quotes/.

Bamberger, M. (2020). "Arnold Palmer's 1960 U.S. Open win was a crowning achievement, and it changed him and the game forever." Golf.com. httsp://golf.com/news/features/arnold-palmer-1960-us-open-changed-game/.

Mell, R. (2020). "From no status to full status, Sophia Popov shocks world with epic Women's Open win." https://www.golfchannel.com/news/no-status-full-status-sophia-popov-shocks-golf-world-epic-womens-open-win.

Joyce, J. (n.d.) Forbes quotes. https://www.forbes.com/quotes/10923/#:~:text=Quotes%20Thoughts%20On%20The%20Business%20Of%20Life&text=A%20man%20of%20genius%20makes%20no%20mistakes.,are%20the%20portals%20of%20discovery.

Workout 29

DiMeglio, S. (2020)."Justin Thomas is going to 'hurt for a while' after painful workday loss." https://golfweek.usatoday.com/2020/07/12/justin-thomas-pga-tour-hurt-painful-workday-loss/.

Green jr. (2020). "Facing difficult test, Spieth trying to ace it." http://read.nxtbook.com/global_golf_post/global_golf_post/20200817/green_col.html?utm_source=newsletter&utm_medium=email&utm_content=READ%20NOW&utm_campaign=dm-081720

Huggan, J. (2020) "Why Tony Jacklin's 1970 U.S. Open win deserves more respect." https://www.golfdigest.com/story/with-50-years-of-perspective-tony-jacklin-looks-back-on-his-1970-us-open-win.

Workout 30

Freakonomics Radio (2018). "Why we choke under pressure and how not to: Featuring Jean Van de Velde." Episode 341. https://freakonomics.com/podcast/choking/.

Nichols, B. (2020). "Mickey Wright in 1963: One of golf's most epic seasons." https://golfweek.usatoday.com/2020/02/21/mickey-wright-1963-golf-most-epic-seasons/.

Gray, W. (2020). "Struggles continue for Jordan Spieth (71) at Wyndham: 'I'm a little uncertain'." https://www.golfchannel.com/news/struggles-continue-jordan-spieth-71-wyndham-im-little-uncertain.

DiMeglia. S. (2021). "Kevin Na closes Sony Open with clutch birdie for fifth PGA Tour title, Brendan Steele lets another slip away." https://golfweek.usatoday.com/2021/01/17/sony-open-kevin-na-pga-tour-title-hawaii/.

Workout 31

Achenbach, J. (2004). "Getting a grip on the yips." https://golfweek.usatoday.com/2004/10/05/2004-getting-grip-yips/

Grand, D. personal communication.

Weinman, S. (2016). "The Shark's Collapse." https://www.golfdigest.com/story/the-sharks-collapse-20-years-later.

Workout 32

Grand, D. & Goldberg, A. (2011). *This is Your Brain on Sports: Beating Blocks, Slumps and Performance Anxiety for Good*! IngramSpark Publishing.

Lightning Source UK Ltd.
Milton Keynes UK
UKHW030628091221
395377UK00006B/450